T0146722

Living in your Fortified Place

Finding Protection in a Troubled World

GLORIA RUSSELL

authorHOUSE®

AuthorHouse™
1663 Liberty Drive
Bloomington, IN 47403
www.authorhouse.com
Phone: 1 (800) 839-8640

Published by AuthorHouse   08/29/2016

ISBN: 978-1-5246-2546-7 (sc)
ISBN: 978-1-5246-2545-0 (e)

Print information available on the last page.

Any people depicted in stock imagery provided by Thinkstock are models,
and such images are being used for illustrative purposes only.
Certain stock imagery © Thinkstock.

This book is printed on acid-free paper.

Because of the dynamic nature of the Internet, any web addresses or
links contained in this book may have changed since publication and
may no longer be valid. The views expressed in this work are solely those
of the author and do not necessarily reflect the views of the publisher,
and the publisher hereby disclaims any responsibility for them.

Scripture quotations marked NKJV are from the Holy Bible, New King James
Version (Authorized Version). First published in 1611. Quoted from the KJV
Classic Reference Bible, Copyright © 1983 by The Zondervan Corporation.

Contents

Foreword vii

Introduction..ix

Chapter 1   Safety First..1

Chapter 2   Power of the Blood................................9

Chapter 3   God's Umbrella of Protection.......................15

Chapter 4   The Spirit of Grace 19

Chapter 5   The Secret Place................................ 28

Chapter 6   Mind Games.................................... 40

Chapter 7   The Place of Prayer............................. 52

Chapter 8   Your Defensive Barrier 66

Chapter 9   The Sphere of God............................. 76

Chapter 10   For The Glory Of God.................................... 83

Chapter 11   The Security of Love....................................... 96

Chapter 12   Understanding God's Covenant of
             Protection 103

Chapter 13 Name of the Lord 111

Chapter 14 War Over Words 115

Chapter 15 Borders and Boundaries 125

Chapter 16 Put On The Lord Jesus Christ 133

Conclusion 145

Foreword

Why would someone be compelled to write a book when there are thousands upon thousands already written? For me the answer is simple. Habakkuk 2:2 tells me, "Write the vision (or revelation-something I see or perceive) and make it plain on tablets(or yellow pads) that he may run who reads it."

As I write this I am in my special place of prayer where I meet with my Lord. When He speaks to me I'm not satisfied until I write it down. Habakkuk said in 2:1, "I will stand my watch." What a precious privilege we have as followers of Jesus Christ to position ourselves before God in prayer and "watch to see what He will say to me."

God speaks! Is that such a surprise?

> **Psalm 119:72, "The law of Your mouth is better to me than thousands of coins of gold and silver."**

What's in your safe? (Sorry! I just broke all the rules of writing, but I just had to say that.)

Today, you can hear God speak to you. He has many things He wants you to know. You will discover a place in God like a multifaceted diamond, a fortified place of peace, power, safety, rest, strength and all the love, protection, and provision you will need for the journey ahead. And best of all, Jesus will meet you there.

Introduction

Walking in the Spirit is the most exciting, adrenalin-pumping life possible on the earth. Think of it! The Almighty Creator God of the Universe walks and talks with His beloved children all the time. Just as He walked with the first man and woman in the Garden, followers of Jesus Christ today have this almost unbelievable opportunity to be in His presence in a personal, intimate relationship called agape love.

The sad truth is we miss much of what God is saying because of unbelief. Then, on rare occasions the Spirit of God surprises us with a unmistakable revelation, speaking in a soft, matter of fact one-liner that goes directly to the heart and soul.

This is what happened recently in an adult Bible class when a substitute teacher casually commented, "You must stay in your fortified place." I doubt if Kathy even remembers saying it, but the Holy Spirit of God drove those seven words to the bull's-eye as far as I was concerned. Since that beautiful Sunday morning I continue to receive more and more revelation of living in God's fortified place. There's much to learn.

Since the writing of my first book, "Surrounded", God has refined this message. I only received "in part" a portion of the revelation but it was life-changing. Today I have received a more thorough understanding of God's covenant of love and protection for His body-those who are in Christ Jesus. As you read this book and continue to walk through the various dimensions of spiritual protection you will have many invitations to stop and worship our wonderful Heavenly Father and to thank Him for keeping you in His fortified place.

It's the right time--the right place, and it's vital to survival. You must stay in God's fortified place!

Definition

The word fortify has two meanings. 1. To make strong or stronger, strengthen physically, emotionally, spiritually. 2. To strengthen against attack.

Another term we understand is the word fort, which is an enclosed place or fortified building for military defense. A fortified place is somewhere you are protected from danger. Or, to have something added that will increase strength, such as a fortified suit of armor.

Each of the definitions are relevant to God's desire ad plan to protect His family.

Chapter One

Safety First

When was the first time you were made aware of the safety of Father God's arms? I was about five years old when my younger sister and I were riding double on Daddy's very gentle, Ole' Babe. The horse got spooked and ran down a steep hill toward home with two frightened little girls hanging on for dear life. After a few minutes I realized I couldn't hold on much longer. I whispered to Barbara who was in front, "Hold on. I'm going." At that moment I was absolutely sure I would soon be with Jesus and everything was going to be alright. Off I went, landing safely in a large sand bed near Hackberry Creek bridge.

Where did this confidence come from? Perhaps it was from this chorus we sang in Sunbeam Class at our little country church.

Safe am I, Safe am I,

In the hollow of His hand.

Sheltered 'ore, Sheltered 'ore

With His love forevermore.

No ill can harm me,

No foe alarm me,

For He keeps both day and night.

Safe am I, Safe am I,

In the hollow of His hand.

Not everyone had the privilege of growing up in church. However, we all have our now time with God. That's what counts. Consider this scripture:

"For He says: In an acceptable time I have heard you, And in the day of salvation I have helped you. Behold now is the accepted time; behold, now is the day of salvation." 2 Corinthians 6:2

Full Salvation

Salvation is the ultimate safety net. The word is huge, being an all-inclusive word signifying forgiveness, healing, prosperity, deliverance, safety, rescue, liberation, and restoration. Salvation becomes a reality only through faith in Jesus Christ. He came into the world for this purpose, that you and I might be forgiven and delivered from the power of sin. Mankind's need for salvation is one of the clearest teachings of the Bible. It is total in scope for the total person: spirit, soul, and body.

Salvation through Jesus Christ is revealed in three tenses: past, present, and future. It is a present possession, with a fuller realization as we continue to walk with Christ.

1. Past: Salvation is past. When a person believes and receives Jesus Christ, he is saved from the penalty of sin, which is eternal separation from God. This is called justification.

   "Believe on the Lord Jesus Christ and you will be saved." Acts 16:31

2. Present: Salvation is present. We are also in the process of being saved from the power of sin as we continue to grow in the grace and knowledge of Jesus. This is known as sanctification.

   "But grow in the grace and knowledge of our Lord and Savior Jesus Christ..." Ephesians 3:18

3. Future: Salvation is future. We shall be saved from the very presence of sin at the coming of our Lord or our home-going to Him. One day our experience of salvation will be complete when Christ returns and the kingdom of God is fully revealed. This is called glorification.

   "Looking for the blessed hope and glorious appearing of our great God and Savior Jesus Christ." Titus 3:13

God's invitation for His salvation is always open:

"For whoever calls on the name of the Lord shall be saved." Romans 10:13

Saving Faith

Once by faith you have the assurance of eternal salvation, you begin to live in complete confidence in our Heavenly Father and what He says He will do for you. Faith is believing what God says in His Word causing you to live for Him in His Presence every day. It is not something you can work up or turn on and off. Faith comes from hearing--really hearing God's take on things and recognizing that He is the Almighty you're not! Growing in the grace and knowledge of our Lord Jesus brings a much stronger sense of protection and safety.

Faith will develop trust. You trust that God is who He says He is and believe He will do exactly what He says He will do. Faith is continuous action from beginning to end--"beginning", meaning when you received Jesus as your personal Savior. The moment you believed Jesus died on the cross, giving His life-blood to pay your sin penalty, that was the moment your faith became active and you received everything God promised, starting with Acts 16:31.

"Believe on the Lord Jesus Christ and you will be saved." Acts 16:31

Faith Grows

From that important beginning faith begins to grow according to the instruction found in 2 Peter 3:18.

"Grow in the grace and knowledge of our Lord and Savior Jesus Christ."

We need to continually check our faith-shield, making sure it's in good working order. We'll learn more about the shield of faith in Chapter Eight. Any hint of doubt or unbelief needs to go. We must focus our effort and energy on getting to know Jesus more and more. This is the primary way to fortify ourselves against the destructive plans of the enemy.

To be safe it is imperative that we make our relationship with Jesus our highest priority--yes, over family, friends, or loved ones. Jesus must have first place.

One of the precious old hymns of the church says, "Jesus, Jesus, how I trust Him, how I've proved Him ore' and ore'. Jesus, Jesus, precious Jesus. Oh, for grace to trust Him more."

Proverbs 10:25 "...whoever trusts in the Lord shall be safe."

Proverbs 18:10 "The name of the Lord is a strong tower; The righteous run to it and are safe."

God reveals Himself in the Scriptures through His many names. These scriptures declare His name as the protection we so desperately need.

The word "safe" implies, "lifted out of reach". How great is that! When you run to the Lord instead of away from Him you have His promise of safety. You can be lifted far above the cares of this world right into His Presence.

A Refuge

Psalm 46:1 "God is our refuge and strength, a very present help in trouble."

Refuge is another word for a fortified place. Webster says the word refuge means shelter or protection from danger or difficulty. Here in Psalm 46, the Psalmist declares that God is our refuge. It is in the safety of His arms we have shelter from the storms of life, help for every need, and comfort in times of great trial or distress.

The Word of God says that those who "have fled (to Him) for refuge" receive mighty indwelling strength and strong encouragement to grasp and hold fast the hope appointed for us and set before us. This hope is a sure and steadfast anchor of the soul that takes us right into the veil of His Presence. How's that for a fortified place! (Hebrews 6: 18,19)

When David prayed in Psalm 31, "...Be my rock of refuge, a fortress of defense to save me," he received the assurance that God answered his cry for help, declaring, "You are my rock and my fortress..."

A similar thought is found in Psalm 125:1. "Those who trust in the Lord are like Mt. Zion which cannot be moved but abides forever." Mt. Zion is a symbol of security. In verse 2, the Psalmist continues.

"As the mountains surround Jerusalem so the Lord surrounds His people from this time forth and forever." Psalm 125:2

Revival Now

Today the church is a city of refuge and an ark of safety for the people of God. If we are to function at our best we, the body of Christ--His church, desperately need revival. This will only be possible if each of us allow revival to begin in me. Paul's cry, "That I may know Him and the power of His resurrection", must become our cry. This should be your greatest desire--to know Him.

There are several things you can do to assure revival in your heart:

- The starting point is intimacy and friendship with God. Understanding the heart of God in friendship brings us into a place of wholeness.

- A revelation of who God has created you to be will refine your identity in Christ.

- Love that allows you to love the Lord with all your heart, and to love His plan for His Kingdom will birth revival.

God is calling His people into the safety of His Presence--a place of refuge where you can walk in intimacy with Him, which is what it means to know Him. It is here in this fortified place with God that our relationship with God is birthed and continues to grow. In this hour when the forces of hell are fighting with their most sophisticated, powerful weapons we must determine to live in God's fortified place of safety.

Chapter Two

Power of the Blood

The Joy Factor

Jesus knew His plight when He entered into the work assigned to Him before the foundation of the world. He knew the price had to be paid-- "the wages of sin is death". He was the only One qualified, sinless and perfect, who could pay the price for the sins of the world--your sins and mine. More than that, He willingly gave His life-blood on the cross with joy. God's Word says that it was for the joy that was set before Him that He endured the torment of the cross. The faithfulness of Jesus to keep His promises is unquestionable. You are the joy that was set before Him.

> *"Looking unto Jesus, the author and finisher of our faith, who for the joy that was set before Him endured the cross, despising the shame and has set down at the right hand of the throne of God." Hebrews 12:2*

This joy was His reality. He could see it--a joy unspeakable and full of glory. If you were the only person in need of forgiveness, He would have died on the cross. That was a done deal before the foundation of the world. Revelation 13:8 says Jesus was crucified before the foundation of the world. Ephesians 1:4 says that God chose you to be in Christ before the foundation of the world. This was God's eternal plan.

The question is when? When would Jesus experience this joy? I'd like to suggest that He lived joy knowing that His purpose and destiny was to save lost humanity. Eternity was in His heart. He knew the end before the beginning. He also knew those who are His. You are in this number if you have trusted Jesus as your Savior from sin. This joy was His always. It was for the "now"--not just for that great day when we all get to Heaven. Jesus is filled with joy over you every day as you walk and talk with Him. Like children, you and I grow up before Him. He loves and cares for us as our Heavenly Father. When we fall He quickly comes to our rescue to pick us up and heal our wounds. He laughs at our silliness, dances with us over our successes. It's all joy!

One of the first revelations of His joy came to me one morning as I was sitting on the living room floor spending time with the Lord. An old hymn began to play out in my mind. I could hear joyful singing: "And He walks with me and He talks with me. And He tells me I am His own. And the joy we share..." The music stopped. I heard the still, small voice of Jesus whisper, "It is a joy 'we' share."

Precious child of God, how I wish I could give you a glowing report of how I handled this encounter.

However, like so many other times in my life I didn't understand it was God's invitation to worship Him. We'll talk about worship later, but for now I can say with all certainty this precious truth of the joy I share with my Lord has never left me. In fact, it gets sweeter and more meaningful with each passing day.

The Blood Atonement

Jesus knew the power behind His blood. This was and is the essential focus of the Scriptures. The satisfaction or payment for human sins was made by the blood of a specified substitute, beginning in Genesis 4:4, when God killed animals to make a covering for Adam and Eve.

> *"For the life of the flesh is in the blood, and I have given it to you upon the altar to make atonement for your souls; for it is the blood that makes atonement for the soul." Leviticus 17:11*

This is the clearest scripture on the necessity of blood. The New Covenant in Christ's blood fulfilled the requirements of the Old Covenant for the redemption of mankind. The blood of Christ satisfied the just demands of God's holy law which decreed, "the wages of sin is death."

Heart Attitude

A sincere desire for relationship continues to be the goal of God's covenant-making activity.

In Matthew 26:28, Jesus transformed the meaning of the elements of the Passover meal into the New. The bread now represented His body, which would be given, and the cup His blood, which would be poured out for the forgiveness of sins. A new and eternal covenant was being established by the blood of Jesus Christ and it is the only means of right relationship with a holy God.

Today, because of the sacrifice of Jesus and the substitutionary death on the cross, "we have redemption through His blood, the forgiveness of sins." (Ephesians 1:7) Jesus' blood brings cleansing, forgiveness and redemption.

The fact that we can receive eternal life and forgiveness of sin by faith in Him is only the first step. That alone is almost too much to take in, but there's more to His story--much more.

I John 1:7 says the blood of Jesus Christ keeps on cleansing us from all sin. Jesus knew that you and I would need His help every day of our lives. This eternal covenant in the blood is a continuous action on God's part to keep us clean all through life so followers of Jesus can stand before Him without fear, having clean hands and a pure heart. This is also part of His story and the joy that was set before Him. Not only are we saved from the death penalty, we can also experience day by day the abundant life He came to give all who will receive Him and live in God's fortified place. The faithfulness of Jesus to keep His promises is unquestionable.

Unbroken Fellowship

Once you accept this revelation perhaps you are ready to know how this word works for you. Most of the time the word explains itself. Let's look at this scripture in its entirety.

> *"If we say that we have fellowship with Him, and walk in darkness, we lie, and do not practice the truth. But if we walk in the light as He is in the light, we have fellowship one with another and the blood of Jesus Christ, His Son cleanses us from all sin." I John 1: 6,7*

The little word "if", gives the first clue. Webster's dictionary says if means a condition or qualification. In other words, there are conditions to most of the promises God has given in His Word. In this case the condition to God's promise of continuous, cleansing from all sin is "if we walk in the light."

Many times light and darkness are used to illustrate a contrast between right and wrong; good and evil; truth and error. To walk in the light means to live a life of holiness and purity. Darkness on the other hand symbolizes error, evil and the works of Satan.

Weapon of Choice

There is another dimension to the blood of Christ in the on-going battle against Satan, represented by a great red dragon.

"And they (God's people) overcame him (the devil) by the blood of the Lamb (Jesus Christ), and by the word of their testimony..." Revelation 12:11

The people of God have been provided a special place of safety in God because of the power of the blood. The primary weapon against our enemy, Satan and his demonic forces, is the blood of the Lamb. The blood provides the body of Christ with every necessary provision to defeat the enemy. We have a place in Christ that prevents Satan from separating us from God's eternal and complete resources: His love, His protection, and His provision. By giving His life Jesus destroyed the devil's work and his plan to annihilate the Church of Jesus Christ.

The "word of our testimony" is our sword in this war against the forces of hell. In Ephesians 6:17, it's called "the sword of the Spirit which is the Word of God." Our testimony is the good news of the Gospel and of the precious blood Jesus gave to save us.

"But thanks be to God who gives us the victory through our Lord Jesus Christ." 1 Corinthians 15:57

Chapter Three

God's Umbrella of Protection

I first heard the concept of God's umbrella many years ago while attending a popular seminar. Since that time several versions of this truth have surfaced.

My take on it is simple. An umbrella has one purpose--to protect. The second point is also simple. You don't have to use your umbrella, and more times than not, you don't, but it's there for your protection.

So the question is, what is God's umbrella of protection? Consider this scripture.

> *"You shall hide them (those who trust in You) in the secret place of Your presence...You shall keep them secretly in a pavilion (shelter)..."*
> *Psalm 31:20*

There is a place in God known as the presence. In verse 21, David compared this place to a fortified city where he found God's kindness and protection.

From the beginning God's desire was to walk and talk with His people. No one knows how long Adam and Eve enjoyed this kind of relationship with God. In the Garden of Eden, they lived in such a perfect place of protection they knew no fear. Instead, they had unbroken fellowship with the great Creator God until sin separated them. Genesis 2:8 says, "Adam and his wife hid themselves from the presence of the Lord God..." Adam explained in v.10, "I heard your voice in the garden, and I was afraid..." Words fail to express the impact of this terrible tragedy. Volumes have been written to help us understand and learn from it. The most important applications are found in the Word itself.

Psalm 66:18 *"If I regard iniquity in my heart the Lord will not hear me."*

Sin separates man from God, removing His umbrella of protection. Many believers today are deceived into believing they are entitled. They sit around making demands for the blessings and favor of God without obedient faith. We do not obey God in order to be rewarded, but we will obey His Word if we are in harmony with God's will and live under the umbrella of His protection. The Holy Spirit who lives in us will manifest His presence outwardly in our life and conduct. To walk according to the Spirit is to follow the desires of the Holy Spirit, to live in a way pleasing to Him. Anyone who does not have the Holy Spirit within is not a Christian. (See Romans 8, for important instruction on this subject.)

Example of Samson

Remember Samson? He was one of the judges God raised up to defeat Israel's enemy, the Philistines. Samson was given incredible physical strength that enabled him to do great exploits. Because of Samson's moral weakness, and the violation of his vows to God, he was discharged from his role as a judge.

One of the saddest verses in the Bible is Judges 16:20. Samson had been tricked by his Philistine lover into revealing the source of his great strength, symbolized by his unshaven hair. While Samson slept she had a man cut off Samson's seven locks of hair that had never been cut.

Then Delilah said, "The Philistines are upon you, Samson!" He woke up thinking he could free himself as he'd done three other times while playing with the enemy, only to discover the presence of the Lord, along with all His strength, was no longer with him. The supernatural power of the Spirit of the Lord had departed and Samson didn't even know it until it was too late.

Numbers 32:23 assures us that sin comes back on you. "...be sure your sin will find you out."

Galatians 6:7, "Do not be deceived, God is not mocked; for whatever a man sows, that he will also reap."

Living in your fortified place you are required to carry the image of Jesus Christ. This means sin will be exposed and dwelt with. Unbelief must be silenced once and for all. Repent, turn around immediately if you are carrying the image of a Savior who fails to confront sin and unbelief in your life. This is truly a false image of God. This deception is very dangerous.

The enemy is looking for anything in your life that would give him a legal right to attack. Sin will expose you for an attack. You must always remember that Satan's plan is to completely destroy you. God's plan is to transform you into the image and likeness of Jesus. Transformation happens as you stay in the fortified place of God's protection.

> ***Ephesians 4: 23,24** "And be renewed in the spirit of your mind and that you put on the new man which was created according to God, in true righteousness and holiness."*

For several years the Holy Spirit has been teaching God's people about the glorious presence of our Lord, reminding us of the possibilities of just how far we can go in God. There is much to learn--more to experience. Jesus sent the Holy Spirit to help you stay focused on Him. Under His umbrella of protection you have everything needed to live a life pleasing to God. The more you know Him the greater your expectancy of getting to know Him even more intimately.

Chapter Four

The Spirit of Grace

Grace is such a beautiful word. For the most part we have a limited understanding of its scope.

I remember a children's musical that attempted to teach grace. One of the lyrics said, grace is not a blue-eyed blond. I recently met one of the most precious, godly women I've known, named Grace. Guess what, she is a blue-eyed blond. I enjoyed having her in the class I was teaching on grace. This may be a silly example, but grace is not what many think.

My first definition of grace was "unmerited favor". When you first receive Jesus as Savior and Lord you receive God's undeserved love and kindness in eternal salvation. This is saving grace.

> *"For by grace you have been saved through faith, and that not of yourselves; it is the gift of God." Ephesians 2:8*

I had been a believer since the age of nine, and I was twenty-one when I first learned of grace. Unmerited favor is still a good definition but like the illustration of a diamond with its many facets, grace will always surprise you when you take another look.

The body of Christ is taking yet another look and receiving grace upon grace--greater grace that we thought possible. This is why after more than sixty years I am still on an upward journey of discovery. Pretty exciting way to live!

Let's consider this passage before we move on:

"But God, who is rich in mercy, because of His great love with which He loved us, even when we were dead in trespasses, made us alive together with Christ (by grace you have been saved), and raised us up together, and made us sit together in the heavenly places in Christ Jesus." Ephesians 2: 4-7.

Grace begins at the cross. This is the ground of all grace--Jesus' death on the cross and the payment in His blood. Because of His great love for us He has cleansed us by the blood, making us holy by His grace.

"In Him we have redemption through His blood, the forgiveness of sins, according to the riches of His grace which He made to abound toward us..." Ephesians 1:7,8a.

Grace is found only in a person, Jesus Christ. It is the "grace of our Lord Jesus Christ." His life was an overflowing demonstration of divine grace and truth.

(John 1:14) To be under grace is to be justified and to live by the indwelling resurrection power of Christ. This is opposite of being under the law, which is trying to earn salvation in your own strength by obeying rules and regulations.

As you observe the "God of all grace", you begin to appreciate all Jesus accomplished in His death and resurrection. It is both humbling and faith-building to be reminded of the majestic diversity of God's grace as it continues to abide with you as the operating power of heaven to meet every need in your life.

Grace is one of those words that carry deep instruction. With each use of the word you are invited to see a greater purpose, or a deeper reality of what it means and how it works in your life. God wants you to have a clear understanding of the perfecting process of grace. It is by His grace that you are perfected and protected.

"Therefore, leaving the discussion of the elementary principles of Christ, let us go on to perfection, not laying again the foundation of repentance from dead works and of faith toward God." Hebrews 6:1

When you begin to speak truth you invite the Teacher, God's Holy Spirit to do His perfecting work in you. Consider what Jesus taught.

"When He, the Spirit of truth, has come, He will guide you into all truth..." John 16:13a

The Golden Grace Key

Recently, as I was preparing to teach on the subject of grace, the Holy Spirit downloaded a new illustration of the simple, yet complex meaning of grace. He showed me a golden master key that every believer receives when they receive Jesus as Savior. I began to see the grace key as it unlocked large, heavy gates to the Kingdom. ("For by grace you have been saved through faith..." Ephesians 2:8) With sins forgiven, washed away and sin's power broken, there's great joy and freedom in unbroken fellowship with the Father and Jesus, God's Son.

"Therefore, having been justified by faith, we have peace with God through our Lord Jesus Christ, through whom also we have access by faith into this grace in which we stand, and rejoice in hope of the glory of God." Romans 5: 12

However, this is just the beginning. I saw a great corridor with many locked doors. In your hand is the golden master key, called Grace, to open every door inside the Kingdom. Each door has a name over the top and each one is designed to perfect and establish you in the faith.

To help you to understand further, ask yourself, "What does a key represent?" A key unlocks and denotes authority. God is ready to give you the desire and the power to do His will. You must simply by faith unlock the door in front of you as it is revealed. Grace will be there just in time with what you need to live a life that pleases God. Grace is God's power for your journey from here to eternity.

The Spirit of Grace

All the blessings and promises of God come from the work of the Holy Spirit in a believer's life. You received the Holy Spirit to help you know exactly what you have been freely given by God.

> *"God has revealed them to us through His Spirit. For the Spirit searches all things, yes, the deep things of God... Now we have received, not the spirit of the world, but the Spirit who is from God, that we might know the things that have been freely given to us by God." 1 Corinthians 2:10,12*

Two elements are necessary if you are to know the things of God.

- Revelation from God by the Spirit
- Agreement with God from the heart

The Door of Revelation

Revelation is divine insight and understanding by the Holy Spirit of the way the Word of God works in your life, which is beyond natural ability to attain.

> *"But as it is written: Eye has not seen, nor ear heard, nor have entered into the heart of man the things which God has prepared for those*

who love Him. But God has revealed them to us through His Spirit..." 1 Corinthians 2:9, 10a

God wants you to know the great and mighty things He has prepared for you. These things are tailor made for each believer according to your particular need. That's why you have been instructed to grow up.

"But grow in the grace and knowledge of our Lord and Savior Jesus Christ..." 2 Peter 3:18a

Perhaps this little acronym for steps to spiritual growth will help in your walk.

G -- Get into His presence and stay there.

R -- Read and meditate on His Word.

O -- Obey what He says.

W -- Worship and adore Him in Spirit and in truth.

Everything begins with revelation on some level. However, revelation must be received by a direct, purposeful decision. You choose to receive a revelation from God by faith.

The Door of Agreement

To agree with God from the heart is to say yes to God's Word, God's will, and God's ways. It is always by grace through faith that we have access into the exceeding riches of His grace.

The words of this powerful little chorus have inspired many to agree with God's plan.

Yes, Lord, yes, to your will and to your way.

Yes, Lord, yes, I will trust You and obey.

When Your Spirit speaks to me,

With my whole heart I'll agree,

And my answer will be yes, Lord, yes.

I have a testimony concerning the power of revelation and personal, positive response to the Spirit of God. It was a time in life when everything was changing. My husband had recently retired after twenty years of military life and our family of six moved home to Texas. The kids were all in school and I planned to return to secretarial work. At the same time, I was somehow being led into serving God.

On this bright, sunny day I was sitting under the dryer at the beauty shop when my attention was drawn to a magazine. The cover pictured tiny footprints on an upward path. The caption read, "Walk Worthy". I quickly turned to the editorial where I found the scripture that changed my life forever.

> *"J, therefore, the prisoner of the Lord, beseech you to walk worthy of the calling with which you were called." Ephesians 4:1*

That's as far as I got before a floodgate of unstoppable tears began to flow as I attempted to hide behind the magazine. Clear revelation filled my mind with a deep understanding of God's call on my life. I immediately said, "Yes". With all that was within me I wanted to obey my God. I also added, "I never want to say no to You again."

I can honestly say that at that time I had no idea what that was all about. I knew it was important to say yes (even before I knew God's will). Little did I know that I was about to enroll in Grace101, which is another class I will never graduate from.

As you come to a greater understanding of living in God's fortified place you will see even more clearly how God's grace is His divine protection and direction for your life and destiny.

Multi-faceted, Many-colored Grace

> *"But grow in the grace and knowledge of our Lord and Savior Jesus Christ..." 2 Peter 3:18*

As you and I continue to seek God and apply the things He says, we will discover more and more about the wonders of God's grace. Grace is part of the spiritual blessings we have in Christ Jesus, and reveals to us the divine privileges and resources available to us today.

I have started writing down definitions of grace as shown to me. Add to this list as you learn more about God's amazing grace.

Grace is:

- Undeserved favor and blessing of God which cannot be worked for or earned and must be received as God's free gift of forgiveness of sin and access into God's presence. (Ephesians 2:8,9)

- The working of God's mighty power to make you joint-heir with Jesus, transforming you into the likeness of His Son.

- Appropriate, timely help coming to do for you what you cannot do for yourself at exactly the right time you need it. (Hebrews 4:16)

- God giving you both the desire and the power to do His will.

- Divine ability to know God and His strategies for bringing His Kingdom to earth.

- God's power to overcome sin in all its forms and manifestations; removes and overcomes every weakness, empowering you to move forward in victory over everything that is not right in you.

Chapter Five

The Secret Place

One of the greatest promises of divine protection is found in Psalm 91. It was written by King David and is most certainly for today. It applies to every believer who will follow the Spirit's instruction found within its words.

As with every promise in the Word of God, there are conditions attached. This Psalm begins with the conditions set forth for a believer to find safety under God's protection.

"He who dwells in the secret place of the Most High shall abide under the shadow of the Almighty." Psalm 91:1

This suggests the greatest assurance of peace and safety is to be at home with God. The secret place is not a place you visit occasionally, such as your favorite vacation spot. To "dwell" in this sense means "to stake your claim". The "he" is you--the one who runs into your fortified place and stays there. You are no longer a visitor, you accept God's invitation to live in His presence 24/7. You are family, a child of the King living under God's protection forever. The promise is "shall abide under the shadow of the Almighty". To abide is to have unbroken fellowship in the Presence of God.

This promise of protection is for anyone who by faith chooses to live in the presence of God. This is the character of a true believer, that you dwell in the secret place of the Most High.

Often young believers live on a daily roller coaster ride. Up and down, in and out of faith, running to God only when they have a need. The rest of the time trying to do it by themselves. Self-sufficiency is a deadly enemy of faith. As you learn to depend completely on God's strength and ability, you will find our all-sufficient God is eternally capable of being all that you need.

"I will say of the LORD, He is my refuge and my fortress, my God, in Him I will trust." Psalm 91:2

Verse 2 is very personal. Every believer must decide, "I will say..." You make an application of God's Word by choosing to identify with it--to own it for yourself.

What you say as a believer has great power. Proverbs 18:21a, "Death and life are in the power of the tongue..." To speak life is to speak God's perspective on any issue of life. To speak God's Word in agreement is to speak life.

Choose to declare the true and living God is your refuge and fortress, your place of protection and safety. This is faith. "In Him I will trust."

The day I learned to say, "I trust You, Lord", was a life-saver for me. Four little words that changes everything: I trust You, Lord! Whether you are in great physical pain, wallowing in self-pity, or overwhelmed with everyday life, when you say with your heart (and mean it), I trust You, Lord, you come into agreement with God's ability to take control. He cannot fail. Regardless of how things look, how you feel, or what others say, you can confidently say, I trust You, Lord. Our God is not a man. He is God. He does not lie. He can be trusted completely. There is no danger of being disappointed in Him. (Numbers 23:19)

Just a word of caution from my personal experience. You may not see things change the way you wanted, but He is always the game changer. When you declare your trust He is faithful to do what He sees as best. In the long run, this is the only safe path. His way is always perfect.

"As for God, His way is perfect; the word of the LORD is proven. He is a shield to all who trust in Him." 2 Samuel 22:31

This confidence in the faithfulness and perfection of God will lead you to declare with absolute certainty, "surely He shall deliver you."

Faith based on a history with God is unshakable. You can yell at the top of your voice, "Look what the Lord has done!" You want everyone to know Him--to find this secret place in God where they can enjoy all the benefits and blessings He gives.

The Psalmist shares his personal experiences of finding help in times of great danger. These are situations or circumstances we all face at one time or another. How wonderful to hold God's promise of protection and safety in our hands.

"Surely He shall deliver you from the snare of the fowler and from the perilous pestilence." (v.3)

This promise of protection from the deadly, unseen trap of the enemy belongs to every generation. We are mostly unaware of the danger of infectious diseases, nor do we always see the effects of sin that we are exposed to on a daily basis. However, God sees and He will defend us in His fortified place.

"He shall cover you with His feathers and under His wings you shall take refuge..."(v.4)

When you go to our Heavenly Father He keeps you safe--hiding you under His protective care. Don't you love the word pictures found here comparing His tender loving care to a hen gathering her chicks under her wings.

"How precious is Your loving kindness O God. Therefore the children of men put their trust under the shadow of Your wings." Psalm 36:7

At Grandma Witt's house chickens were an important part of their daily provision. It was an on-going battle to keep the chickens safe from chicken hawks and chicken snakes. A mother hen is very protective gathering her young under her wings at the first sign of danger. Of course, Grandpa Witt's shotgun was always handy, just in case.

"His truth shall be your shield and buckler." (v.4)

God is gentle and merciful, loving and caring for each of His children. He is also all-powerful and as a man of war He defends you. In His truth you can find a safe zone. It is something you can stake your life on.

"You shall not be afraid..." (v.5)

How could you be afraid when you know that God is with you? He has promised that He will never leave you nor forsake you. (Hebrew 13:5)

For centuries believers have found great comfort in the six little verses of Psalm 23. In verse 4, David declares "Yea, though I walk through the valley of the shadow of death, I will fear no evil..." Then, in awe and wonder he directs his thoughts to God, "For You are with me..."

How can you ward off fear when it suddenly comes at you and catches you off guard?

"Therefore submit to God. Resist the devil and he will flee from you. Draw near to God and He will draw near to you..." James 4:7,8a

You don't wait for fear to show up. You must begin now to get as close to God as possible. Acknowledge His presence. That's one of the reasons the Lord sent God the Holy Spirit to live inside every believer. He is there to help you. Confess out loud, "Lord, You are with me. I will not be afraid."

"There is no fear in love, but perfect love casts out fear, because fear has torment. But he who fears has not been made perfect in love." I John 4:18

Knowing and possessing God's love results in fearless confidence toward God and man. You must receive God's love by faith as you do all things pertaining to God. He said he loves you with an everlasting love. That's that! Today we stand before God without fear. By faith we receive the love of God in Christ Jesus and stand against fear.

"You shall not be afraid" (v.5,6)

- *of the terror by night*
- *nor the arrow that flies by day*
- *nor of the pestilence that walks in darkness*
- *nor of the destruction that lays waste at noonday*

In God's fortified place, with God's love and protection we are not afraid of the unseen dangers of night or day.

"A thousand may fall at your side, and ten thousand at your right hand, but it shall not come near you." (v.7)

When you see death and destruction in the physical our natural human response is fear. However, looking at the bigger picture we understand how Jesus can promise this word.

"Most assuredly, I say to you, if anyone keeps My word he shall never see death." John 6:47

To establish this promise further we have only to look at the words, everlasting and eternal. This speaks of something above and beyond the limitations of time, having no beginning or without end, lasting forever.

Man is more than a physical creature. He is also a spiritual being. Physical death does not mean the end of existence but is simply the transition to another dimension in which our conscious existence continues. For a follower of Jesus Christ this means we move into our heavenly home to be with our Lord forever. For those without Christ it means eternal punishment in hell.

"Only with your eyes shall you look and see the reward of the wicked..." (v.8)

We are not sure exactly how this word will be played out in the future, but today there is no question about it. It is easy to see the destruction that surrounds those without Christ, who do not live in God's fortified place of protection.

"Because you have made the Lord, who is my refuge, even the Most High, your dwelling place, no evil shall befall you, nor shall any plague come near your dwelling."(v.9,10)

What a great and precious promise for all who live in God's fortified place of safety in the secret place. You have divine protection because you are continually with God and rest in Him. Regardless of what happens to you, nothing can hurt you. This promise even provides divine protection for where you live.

"For He shall give His angels charge over you, to keep you in all your ways. In their hands they shall bear you up, lest you dash your foot against a stone." (v.11,12)

When it comes to the subject of God's powerful heavenly host, called angels, I have only one word of caution: Stay with the Scriptures! Don't allow the world's ideas to dictate your belief-system, especially when it comes to the heavenly hosts of angels, created long before man and assigned to serve God and to protect the body of Christ (His Church).

Angels are quite real. Although mostly invisible they clearly play a vital role in the life of every believer. This is just another spiritual blessing and great advantage you experience living in the secret place.

Most of us can remember a time when without angelic help you would have surely had a terrible accident, or worse. Some of these incidents are very serious, and many may seem small, but how thankful we are for the reality of this powerful promise that God sends angels to partner with us.

"You shall tread upon the lion and the cobra, the young lion and the serpent you shall trample under foot." (v.13)

In Luke 10:19, Jesus announced to His followers in similar symbolic language saying, "Behold, I give you the authority to trample on serpents and scorpions, and over all the power of the enemy, and nothing shall by any means hurt you."

Serpents and scorpions are symbols of spiritual enemies and demonic powers over which Jesus has given His followers authority. Victory over the powers of darkness depend upon living in God's fortified place of safety. In this secret place we have nothing to fear from man or beast.

"Because he has set his love upon Me, therefore I will deliver him, I will set him on high, because he has known my name." (v.14)

Paul expressed his desire to know God, saying, "That I may know Him and the power of His resurrection..." (Philippians 3:10) His pursuit of knowing God was based on his love for God. His focus was on knowing in the

deepest, most intimate relationship possible. Paul knew who he was in Christ and that he had no claim to fame other than the righteousness he received by faith in Jesus Christ.

To set your love upon God means that you will become like Him, reflecting His love through your life-style. We may not fully know the nature of God but He has revealed Himself by His Name, which we must get to know.

I love the promise here to "set you on high". In the secret place of God's presence we are raised to a new level of protection, far out of reach of trouble.

"He shall call upon Me, and I will answer him..." (v.15)

God responds to His people when we pray. The best prayer is dialogue, not monologue. He hears and He answers! That's the promise found here. The Father wants to hear your voice from His fortified place. He pours out upon you the spirit of prayer according to His will and when you pray, He answers. Every believer can become God's partner-in-prayer.

"I will be with him in trouble..." (v.15b)

When our Heavenly Father says, "I will...", you can believe it. If God speaks a word He will certainly bring it to pass.

"Indeed, I have spoken it. I will bring it to pass, I have purposed it, I will also do it." Isaiah 46:11.

This is God's solemn word and a precious promise when He says, "I will".

"I will be with Him..." Stop right there. Could there be a more important promise than this? Father God says, "I will be with you." In Hebrews 13:5, we learn the rest of the story. "For He Himself has said, I will never leave you nor forsake you."

You are never alone in God's fortified place. You have a place in God that cannot be taken away. He is there.

"I will deliver him and honor him." (v.15b)

You and I have the greatest privilege offered to a human being--to be honored by God. Think of it! Almighty God, Creator of everything has chosen you. You belong to Him through faith in Jesus Christ. What an honor!

"Behold what manner of love the Father has bestowed on us, that we should be called children of God..." I John 3:1.

"...With long life I will satisfy him and show him My salvation."(v.16)

How long is long? One thing we've learned is that God's way of measuring is not man's way.

God says, "One day is as a thousand years and a thousand years as one day." (2 Peter 3:8) God says, "How could one chase a thousand and two put ten thousand to flight..."(Deuteronomy 32:30) We must simply agree-- "Yes and amen"!

Whatever life has been designated to you will be more than enough. You will be satisfied when you see our precious Lord and Savior and the completion of salvation's plan.

Our place today is to stay in the safety of God's protection in the secret place. We need no other. This is to live in your fortified place.

Chapter Six

Mind Games

The mind is the part of a person that thinks, reasons, and understands. Sometimes it is referred to as soul, as David used in Psalm 23.

"He restores my soul..." Psalm 23:3

At other times, heart, as in this verse.

"A sound heart is life to the body..." Proverbs 14:30a

The mind has often been called a battlefield for good reason. Life can be brutal. Life can be blessed. Both are true, are they not? One may refer to the glass as half full, while another would say it is half empty.

Perception often becomes your reality. Could this be the reason God instructs us to think on good things and positive things in Philippians 4:8? The wise writer of Proverbs observed, "For as he thinks in his heart, so is he..." Proverbs 23:7a It would be smart to take his advice and guard your mind.

Scientists have said that the average person uses only 10 percent of his mind's capabilities during his lifetime. When it comes to learning, everything you see, hear, touch, and smell is recorded primarily through the eyes and ears. Although most of this data cannot be recalled at will, it is there nonetheless to dictate how you think. How you think will determine the way you live.

Therefore, it is important for spiritual vitality to control what you see, what you hear and how you think because whatever you see or hear influences your mind, which in turn affects your emotions or feelings. Feelings are not spontaneous. You control them by controlling your mind. When the emotions become activated this will determine the action you will take because of these thoughts and emotions.

Why is this important? Your life here and your eternal destiny are determined by the mind--what you think in your mind; your emotions-- how you feel; and your will-- what you do or the decisions you make. You cannot undervalue protection of your mind.

Here are several important areas where the battle for the mind rages:

Fear V.S. Faith

It's really quite amazing how the mind works. One thought leads to another and another in an upward spiral into the very presence of God, or a downward spiral right into the quicksand that will swallow you up.

41

The ultimate answer to combating fear is to be growing in faith. As you learn to defeat fear, your faith will grow by leaps and bounds. If you do not control your mind fear will take you over.

> *"There is no fear in love, but perfect love casts out fear, because fear involves torment. But he who fears has not been made perfect in love."*
> *1 John 4:18*

This scripture explains how fear brings thoughts of well-deserved punishment. When your confidence is in God you can stand up under difficult circumstances. Consider the following faith boosters:

- Determine in your heart to stay in the love of God. Love secures your heart. When the spirit of fear attacks and you feel helpless to defend yourself get into the habit of putting a stop to thoughts that are against or contrary to the knowledge of God. Turn it around and run to Christ with heartfelt thankfulness and praise. His perfect love will cast out fear and you will have experienced another awesome opportunity to get back into God's fortified place of protection.

- Defeat self-talk by getting rid of negative thoughts of yourself and other, negative habits, or any belief that doesn't help you succeed.

- Get cleaned up from mental dirt. The wisdom of Proverbs tells us that what you think in your heart is who you are. (Proverbs 23:7a)

The Peace of God

I'm sure you've used the term, "peace of mind". It means to be free from disturbance, agitation, or to be at peace. Many in the medical profession believe this state of being at peace is healthy both physically as well as spiritually.

When David wrote Psalm 23, He was making a declaration of facts he knew from personal experience. One of the things he said in verse three is extremely important to us today.

> *"He restores my soul, He leads me in the paths of righteousness for His name's sake."*

Daily restoration of the mind is a major human need as we've already stated. It's only available to those who stay in God's fortified place in the peace of God. We have further instruction in the New Testament.

> *"Let the peace of Christ rule in your hearts..."*
> *Colossians 3:15*

In the battle for peace there's usually an argument going on in your mind: "Should I do this or would that be better? Do I move or should I stay put? Can I speak my mind or must I be silent."

For the follower of Christ the Holy Spirit uses peace to communicate with us. If the situation needs caution, our peace is troubled. If you make a right decision, peace confirms it. This becomes extremely important when life-changing decisions must be made. It's up to you to let the peace of Christ control your thoughts and emotions. When you are grounded in God's Word you can trust peace, along with the Word, to be your guide. This inner witness of God's Spirit protects you from bad choices and wrong decisions.

The Word of God

Since the Garden of Eden mankind has struggled with who will control the mind--man or God. Every human problem is the result of mankind thinking they know better than God. With man in control life is in constant turmoil. When you surrender control of your life to God and live according to His Word, you will find answers to problems and a safe haven--a fortified place of safety, comfort, and refuge. The Word becomes a spiritual map leading you into the life you were created for.

What controls the beliefs in your heart? This, along with words of agreement with God's Word will change your life and affect your circumstances. God said it! I believe it! That settles it!

> *"And do not be conformed to this world, but be transformed by the renewing of your mind..."*
> *Romans 12:2*

> *"And be renewed in the spirit of your mind."*
> *Ephesians 4:23*

If the mind is to be renewed you absolutely must read and meditate on the Word of God. There is no Plan B. Consider what Jesus said in John 6.

> *"...The words that I speak to you are spirit, and they are life." John 6:63b*

Recently, I was reminded of scripture I had previously rejected. We all tend to look into the word through our carefully crafted filter of pride or intellect or religion. We may even have the audacity to say, "That can't be true!" or, "I'm sure God doesn't mean that," or, "I think that means..." Please don't misunderstand what I am saying. It's good--even necessary to examine the Word of God to discover root meanings, word definitions and to seek understanding in light of the context of a scripture. It's only after careful study and seeking the Holy Spirit's instruction that you can know the truth that will set you free. (John 8:32)

> *"Every word of God is pure and is a shield to those who put their trust in Him. Do not add to His words, lest He rebuke you, and you be found a liar." Proverbs 30: 5,6*

What is the solution to this and many other mind games? We have discovered the importance of controlling the mind, now we need to know how this is possible. Our thinking processes must be transformed or we will continue thinking with a carnal mind that cannot understand the way God thinks. I want to suggest three possibilities:

1. Obedient faith.

   "Therefore lay aside all filthiness and overflow of wickedness, and receive with meekness the implanted word, which is able to save your souls. But be doers of the word, and not hearers only, deceiving yourselves." James 1: 21,22

   God's goal for growing in grace and knowledge of our Lord Jesus through prayer, church attendance, worship and Bible study is a transformed life that results in a life of service that honors God.

2. Your mind renewed to the Word of God.

   "And do not be conformed to this world, but be transformed by the renewing of your mind, that you may prove what is that good and acceptable and perfect will of God." Romans 12:2

   Renewing of the mind is the work of the Holy Spirit in your life. Here it suggests a complete change of heart and life for the better and an adjustment of one's moral and spiritual vision.

3. The mind of Christ.

   "You have the mind of Christ."

   God wants the thoughts of Christ to flow freely into your conscious mind. Keep saying, "I have the mind of Christ", until it becomes a reality.

Flesh V.S. Spirit

We have a warning in God's Word to be constantly on guard--stay alert. This is no time to mess around. If you are to stay in the fight you need two things. This will prepare you to be armed and dangerous in the coming season.

"But put on the Lord Jesus Christ and make no provision for the flesh to fulfill its lusts."
Romans 13:14

1. To "put on the Lord Jesus" is to live in unbroken fellowship, submitting to the Holy Spirit's control, and depending on His strength. Jesus said, "The flesh is weak." (Matthew 26:41)

2. "Make no provision for the flesh" means to control sensual desires and appetites by starving it. Don't encourage the self-centered life of your past by catering to impulses of the carnal nature.

For further help in the battle against the flesh we need a deeper understanding of this powerful enemy.

"I say then, walk in the Spirit, and you shall not fulfill the lust of the flesh. For the flesh lusts against the Spirit, and the Spirit against the flesh, and these are contrary to one another, so that you do not do the things that you wish."
Galatians 5: 16,17

To walk implies forward movement or steady progress in spiritual growth in Christ Jesus. We are to be constantly living in the Spirit. The word Spirit (Holy Spirit) suggests a sphere and can be pictured as a dot inside a circle. We are to constantly live in the circle of God's love, His protection, and His provision as provided here by the Holy Spirit of God. (See Chapter Nine -- The Sphere of God).

You have a precious promise in this scripture, that if you obey the indwelling Spirit--do what He tells you to do, yielding to Him for His divine energy needed to do it, you will not fulfill the cravings of the fallen nature.

In verse 17, we see the battle is on. You simply cannot water down this truth. The fleshly nature is at war against the Holy Spirit of God.

The work of the Holy Spirit is to put sin out of your life and to produce His own fruit: love, joy, peace, longsuffering, kindness, goodness, faithfulness, gentleness, self-control. When the Spirit fully controls the life of a believer He produces all of these graces.

The work of the flesh or fallen nature is to stop any progress you make through the Holy Spirit's power and influence.

The word "contrary" speaks of this war between flesh and Spirit. The word meaning pictures two opposing armies. Each digging trenches to hold their ground and fight to the finish.

This mind-game is going on in the heart of every believer. Thanks be to God, He has given you the key to victory.

Pride V.S. Humility

The definition of pride is haughtiness or arrogance. It means you exalt your own ideas above God and others. Pride is an attitude of superiority. By the way, it's important to remember that pride is on God's list of things that defile His people.

Kick pride out--pride of your own beliefs, your own denomination, your own family, your own race or party. Spiritual and political pride have no place in God's perfect plan for your life. Pride is your enemy and will stop the move of God that will take you to a higher level.

Humility is to recognize the power and strength you possess is from God and to be thankful. This is when you are the strongest and most powerful.

"...God resists the proud but gives grace to the humble. Therefore, humble yourselves under the mighty hand of God that He may exalt you in due time." J Peter 5:5b, 6

Conditions and Promises

"But without faith it is impossible to please Him, for he who comes to God must believe that He is, and that He is a rewarder of those who diligently seek Him." Hebrews 11:6

While it may be possible to recognize your need to meet the qualification of love, obedient faith, walk in the Spirit and other things the Word of God sets forth for you to follow and even pray often about these important commands, we often reject the great and precious promises attached, which are the rewards of the faithful and the result of our covenant with God. This is a mystery to me, nonetheless true.

You probably had no problem with Acts 16:31, receiving this truth into your heart for salvation. You believed on Jesus, and you are saved. You are absolutely sure because the Word of God says so. This is truly a great and mighty promise and you met the condition, to believe.

What about God's promises to bless you, to answer prayer, to lead you, to meet your needs, to give you strength and health and vitality? It is possible to miss what God wants to do for you simply because you do not know what His precious promises are and how they apply to the rewards God wants to give you today. Remember, God rewards the faithful.

Who Am I?

One of the loudest, most boisterous voices you will hear is when the enemy wants to question your salvation, or God's plan for your life. He works hard to fill your thoughts with your weaknesses, your failures, your inadequacies, or your questionable motives.

In the days ahead you must learn to tune out the voice of the enemy, release all wrong ideas of who you think you are and embrace who He is in you and what God says about you in His Word. God wants you to see yourself through His eyes, trust what He shows you, and walk in obedient faith. For this to become a reality in your life you need a clearer understanding of His Presence and power.

"By having the eyes of your heart flooded with light, so that you can know and understand the hope to which He has called you, and how rich is His glorious inheritance in the saints (His set-apart ones) and [so that you can know and understand] what is the immeasurable and unlimited and surpassing greatness of His power in and for us who believe, as demonstrated in the working of His mighty strength." Ephesians 1: 18,19 Ampli.

Chapter Seven

The Place of Prayer

As we have discovered, to live in God's fortified place is a much-to-be-desired state of being. Protection is one of man's most basic needs.

One of the definitions of fortified is having something added to increase strength. This is prayer power provided by the indwelling Holy Spirit of God.

There is a war being waged for the Kingdom of God. You, precious believer, were drafted into God's army the very day you received Christ. All who belong to Jesus fight on our knees in prayer.

What Next?

A great woman of God once said, "All difficulties in prayer can be traced to one cause: praying as if God were absent."

In pre-school you and I were taught a very important lesson on prayer. Prayer is talking to God. Today you may still be asking, "Where is God?" Many of us have no problem believing God is in Heaven, but to believe

He is in the here and now, well, that's another thing altogether. What about living in you?

When you begin to ask, as Jesus' disciples did, "Teach us to pray", you're off to a great start. First, you must acknowledge He is here. Prayer is not talking to yourself, or to the air, or the ceiling. Prayer is communicating with our living God as you would talk to your best friend. He has promised not only to be with you, but never to leave you nor forsake you. (Hebrews 13:5b)

Further proof of God's abiding presence is found in one of the ways God reveals Himself to us and that is through His name, Jehovah-Shammah, which means, "The Lord is There". The most precious promise believers can receive is the presence of our God through the indwelling Holy Spirit who Jesus said would be in us forever as Helper. (John 14: 16,17)

Hedge of Protection

Prayer creates hedges of protection that keep you and your loved ones safe. The Word of God gives clear instruction on how to overcome the enemy of our soul. Prayer is the battle and the Word of God is your weapon of choice. You will never win in this life without prayer. It is quite scriptural to pray a hedge of protection around a loved one or church member.

Bringing Down Strongholds

"For though we walk in the flesh, we do not war according to the flesh. For the weapons of our warfare are not carnal but mighty in God for pulling down strongholds, casting down arguments and every high thing that exalts itself against the knowledge of God, bringing every thought into captivity to the obedience of Christ." 2 Corinthians 10: 3-5

Through prayer you can bring down strongholds that have been established in the mind. A stronghold refers to wrong thinking which allows demonic activity to attack. It is a mindset impregnated with hopelessness that will cause you to accept as unchangeable situations that you know are not God's will. "Taking every thought captive", is a life or death issue that you must learn to deal with. (see Chapter 6)

The Three Enemies

You noticed I said, "enemies", plural. There are three distinct enemies we are at war against: the devil, a fallen angel; the world system that works in opposition to God's Word, God's will, and God's ways; and the flesh, which is the carnal nature wanting to stay in control.

- the devil

"Be sober, be vigilant, because your adversary the devil walks about like a roaring lion, seeking whom he may devour." I Peter 5:8

In order to stand against intimidating demonic resistance you must first submit to God. He promises victory when you apply two principals from James 4:7.

"Therefore submit to God. Resist the devil and he will flee from you." James 4:7

To submit is to fully embrace the Lord Jesus in complete dependence and trust and in full obedience to His Word, His will and His ways. By submitting to God you come into agreement with what God says and fully reject lies of the enemy.

To resist is a military term that indicates standing firm against the enemy. We must be spiritually alert to withstand the attacks against us by prayer and spiritual warfare. To help win this battle against Satan, God has provided the power of Christ's blood and the authority of His Word on our lips. (Revelations 12:11)

"But the Lord is faithful, who will establish you and guard you from the evil one." 2 Thessalonians 3:3

"And they (the followers of Jesus) overcame him (the devil) by the blood of the Lamb (Jesus Christ) and by the word of their testimony (the Word of God), and they did not love their lives to the death (even when faced with death)." Revelation 12:11

God has declared His body righteous and victorious through the blood of Christ. (Colossians 1:20) The death of Christ restored all that had been lost in the Garden. The enemy hates nothing more than the blood of Christ. The blood stands as a permanent declaration of Satan's defeat. Use it against him. Quote scriptures about the blood and see the enemy flee. By appropriating the victory of the finished work of the cross, "the blood of the Lamb", and obedient faith and declaration of the promise and authority of God's Word, you will overcome all the power of the enemy. The word of our testimony is the Word of God on our lips. The Word is referred to as a sword for very good reason. It is powerful and sharper than any two-edged sword.

- the world

In the New Testament this word "world" is often speaking of a world system alienated from and enemy of God over which the evil one rules.

> ***"We know we are of God, and the whole world lies under the sway of the wicked one." I John 5:19***

Peter wrote a very applicable scripture in I Peter 4:3, saying that we spent enough of our past lifetime doing the things the world dictates. Now that we are no longer of the world he writes in 4:7, that we must be serious and watchful in our prayer.

The fact of warfare between the world system and the Kingdom of God is not disputed by active followers of Jesus Christ. We are the ones who seek His Kingdom first, and our goal is to bring the reality of God's Kingdom into our world.

The battle rages as we pray. We must be battle-ready at all times. We'll cover how to be prepared in Chapter Eight.

- the flesh

This term refers to the fallen nature of man with its lusts and desires.

"...Walk in the Spirit, and you shall not fulfill the lust of the flesh. For the flesh lusts against the Spirit..." Galatians 5: 16,17

This enemy, the flesh, is at war with anyone who desires to live a life under the control of and empowered by the Holy Spirit. Growth in Christ increases resistance to all that is against Christ as you learn to walk in the Spirit.

It would be difficult to live under the Holy Spirit's control without acknowledging who the Spirit is. There seems to be much fear and confusion about the Person of the Holy Spirit.

Do not be afraid of the Holy Spirit. He is God just as Father is God and Jesus, God's Son is God. There are three manifestations of our one and only God. They are co-equal in rank and power in the Godhead, with no jealousy or competition between them. This was true before the foundation of the world in eternity past and continues to be true today, as God does not change.

"For J am the Lord, J do not change..." Malachi 3:6a

"Therefore do not be unwise, but understand what the will of the Lord is...be filled with the Spirit." Ephesians 5: 17,18b

The tense of the Greek for "be filled" makes clear that the Spirit-filled condition does not stop with a single experience, but is maintained by continually "be being filled". The Spirit is to influence all aspects of our lives, overflowing with power into our prayer life and defeating all enemies.

Seed Faith

Prayer is like planting seeds. You pray and believe and the Spirit of God watches over that seed to see it germinate and grow.

One morning in prayer I had a vision of a book before me. The pages began to slowly turn so I could see each one. On each page was a picture of a different flower with complete instructions on how to prepare for planting, when and where to plant, and how to care for each one according to its particular needs. I knew this book belonged to God and each of His children were represented by one of the flowers.

In planting seeds of faith when you pray, you are partnering with the purposes of heaven for God's will to be done on earth as it is in heaven. God watches over the seeds of prayer as He does each of His children and answers each one perfectly. To believe this is to pray in faith, without which you cannot please God.

God knows exactly how to take our tiny prayer seeds and with careful working behind life's circumstances He watches over His work to completion according to His perfect will.

> *"Now may He who supplies seed to the sower, and bread for food, supply and multiply the seed you have sown and increase the fruits of your righteousness." 2 Corinthians 9:10*

All Kinds of Prayer

> *"Praying always with all prayer and supplication in the Spirit, being watchful to this end with all perseverance and supplication for all the saints." Ephesians 6:18*

Perhaps you did not realize that God has given many different kinds of prayer for your war chest. Life's battles must be waged in prayer.

Just as American soldiers are trained and equipped with many different types of weapons to use on the battlefield, God's army is also prepared for spiritual warfare by learning to use all forms of prayer. This is how you engage the enemy--with all kinds of prayer. The one you use depends on the need.

- Continual attitude of prayer

"Pray without ceasing." I Thessalonians 5:17

I mention this type of prayer first because of the inclusive nature of this command. Prayer for a sincere seeker should be as natural as breathing. Recognizing that you have unbroken fellowship with God and complete dependence upon Him in everything you do keeps you in an attitude of prayer. You will always keep on praying and refuse to allow anything to keep you from talking to your Heavenly Father.

There's an important truth essential to an effective prayer life that you need to remember: God is not angry. He is not mad at you. You need to allow this word to go deep into your spirit. God loves you. He desires a relationship with you and waits for you to call on His Name.

"Behold, I stand at the door and knock. If anyone hears My voice and opens the door, I will come in to him and dine with him, and he with Me." Revelation 3:20

- Prayer of Repentance

Live a repentant lifestyle bringing personal sin to God for forgiveness. Psalm 66:18 is a very stern warning for every believer. Unconfessed sin builds a dividing wall between you and God. Be thankful for the blood that keeps on cleansing you from all sin.

> *"If I regard iniquity in my heart the Lord will not hear." Psalm 66:18*

> *"If we say that we have no sin, we deceive ourselves, and the truth is not in us. If we confess our sins, He is faithful and just to forgive us our sins and to cleanse us from all unrighteousness." I John 1:9*

God always hears the prayer of a truly repentant person. His faithfulness to forgive and to cleanse you is a solemn promise He makes to anyone who will agree with Him in repentance.

- Prayer of Forgiveness

Forgive anyone who has offended you. Adopt forgiveness of others into your prayer life so God will forgive you.

> *"For if you forgive men their trespasses your heavenly Father will also forgive you." Matthew 6:14*

- Prayer of Adoration

Expressions of love in response to God's great love should drive your prayer life. I'm sure you have used the little chorus, "I Love You, Lord", to express your deepest feelings of love for our Lord. This is a prayer of adoration.

- Prayer of Thanksgiving

"Continue earnestly in prayer being vigilant in it with thanksgiving." Colossians 4:2

Be thankful. Thanksgiving comes from a grateful heart that acknowledges all God has done for you.

- Prayer of Praise

God's people are the only ones who can tell of God's value and worth. Praise Him. Let everything you do be a praise to Him. Come into His presence with praise when you pray. Worship and thanksgiving should accompany all prayer.

"Enter into His gates with thanksgiving, and into His courts with praise. Be thankful to Him, and bless His name." Psalm 100:4

- Dedication and Consecration

Pray for yourself, submitting your personal needs before the throne room. You have been invited to enter and to remain there for help with all your needs. Renew your commitment today. Consecrate yourself to God by drawing a circle around yourself and giving everything inside the circle completely to God for Him to use as He wills.

"Let us therefore come boldly to the throne of grace, that we may obtain mercy and find grace to help in time of need." Hebrews 4:16

- Intercessory Prayer

Pray for the needs of others as the Holy Spirit brings individuals to your mind. Write requests as they are received so you won't forget. This is the greatest expression of love you can give to another person. These prayer assignments may come through phone conversations, dreams, or other as the Spirit of God wills.

- Spiritual Warfare

Aggressive prayer warfare attacks demonic strongholds. Put on and keep on the armor of God so you can stand against the enemy and keep on standing, ready for the next battle. (See Chapter 8)

"Finally, my brethren, be strong in the Lord and in the power of His might. Put on the whole armor of God that you may be able to stand against the wiles of the devil." Ephesians 6: 10,11

- Prophetic Intercession

Recently the Holy Spirit spoke into my spirit, "Cast your net!" In my mind's eye I immediately saw a large net being thrown out over the water. Every time I say the words, cast your net, I see this beautiful picture.

As I prayed for revelation and understanding God showed me step by step a strategy for victory that I am to communicate to Christian leaders for the season ahead.

As you pray according to God's will you can expect God to answer. He has given you delegated authority over your assigned area and sphere of influence. You can expand your sphere of influence and outreach ability with a prayer-net.

God says, cast your net over your family, your home and property, your church, your workplace. Cast your net! Cast your net over that difficult situation facing you with obedient faith and prayer and see God's miraculous answers.

Closet Prayer

> *"But you, when you pray, enter into your closet, and when you have shut the door, pray to your Father who is in secret; and your Father, who sees in secret, shall reward you openly."*
> *Matthew 6:6*

The movie, "War Room", has given new meaning to the prayer closet. Many believers today actually pray in a special set-apart place. This kind of prayer life is easier said than done. It requires that you make a determined effort to make room in your busy life to spend time alone with the Lord. Once established this most important time must be maintained and constantly contended for. God's promise to all who respond to this instruction is to reward you. Your reward will soon be obvious as His answers to your prayers come pouring in.

Jesus gave us an example of the importance of special, private times with God. He got up early, before daylight, and went out alone to a private place where He prayed. (Mark 1:35)

Promises of Answered Prayer

"Now this is the confidence that we have in Him, that if we ask anything according to His will, He hears us. And if we know that He hears us whatever we ask, we know that we have the petitions that we have asked of Him." I John 5: 14,15

Jesus gave us a condition to this great and precious promise. (See Chapter 13)

"If you ask anything in My name I will do it." John 14:14

Stones of Remembrance

By recording answered prayer you can set up stones of remembrance that will testify of God's goodness forever. As stones of remembrance accumulate over your lifetime, your faith becomes actual knowledge. You know personally the goodness of God and His faithfulness because of your relationship with Him and the many personal encounters and answered prayer. In this way you will be His witness to those who need to hear.

Chapter Eight

Your Defensive Barrier

If you were misled about what life would be like as a follower of Jesus Christ with words such as, "Everything will be alright", or "All your troubles will be over", etc., it didn't take long for reality to set in, right?

This reality is that while you may be changed and have new life in Christ, your deadly enemies have not changed. In fact, now they are stirred up like disturbing a wasp nest--which is something we can relate to here in East Texas where I live.

As we have discovered, to live in God's fortified place is a much-to-be-desired state of being. Protection is one of man's most basic needs and it is a daily need rather than an occasional one.

Fortification

The word fortify has two meanings. 1. To make strong or stronger, strengthen physically, emotionally, spiritually. 2. To strengthen against attack. Another term you may understand is the word fort, which is an enclosed place or fortified building for military defense.

A fortified place is somewhere you are protected from danger. Or, to have something added that will increase strength, such as a fortified suit of armor.

There is a war being waged for the Kingdom of God. You, precious believer, were drafted into God's army the very day you received Christ. You will learn to fight this spiritual warfare on your knees in prayer.

Important Question

It may be important at this point to ask yourself, what is spiritual warfare?

1. Spiritual warfare is first of all position. "In Christ" clearly places you in the circle of God's protection made possible through the power of the cross. The good news is that since you are now "in Christ", you have been placed in authority over the power of darkness and all your soul's enemies. This delegated authority can only be asserted, demonstrated, and sustained through spiritual warfare. You have victory because you are in Christ, our victorious warrior and commander of heaven's armies. There isn't anything you can't do when you're in Christ. There isn't any darkness you can't invade with His light. There's nothing too dark, nothing too evil, nothing too strong for the Lord who by His Spirit lives in you.

As any good soldier knows you do not decide when you are on duty. To leave your post is to be A.W.O.L.

(Absent Without Leave). The body of Christ does not have the luxury of being a soldier one day and an actor the next. You are to be on call twenty-four hours a day, seven days a week. You must stay in position and battle ready at all times.(1 Peter 5:8)

2. <u>Spiritual warfare is praise</u>. Declaring the worthiness of our God in praise strikes a blow to the enemy. Satan hates God with a fiery passion. The last thing he wants to see is the people of God worshiping our Heavenly Father. Demons flee when the sound of praise fills the air because God is there.

   "But You are holy, enthroned in the praises of Israel." Psalm 22:3

   Worship is the key to entering fully into God's presence. The word "enthroned" means that when God's people exalt Him, praise invites the ruling presence of God onto the scene.

   A popular chorus from not too long ago says: Praise Him in the morning, praise Him in the evening, praise Him when I'm young and when I'm old...praise Him!

   Worship and praise is a response we should have to God when He reveals Himself to us. David must have hit the devil hard with his praises to God. You and I have an open invitation to join him in the fight.

"Among the gods there is none like You, O Lord, nor are there any works like Your works. All nations whom You have made shall come and worship before You, O Lord, and shall glorify Your name. For You are great, and do wondrous things. You alone are God." Psalm 86: 8-10

The organized church is the only place in America where you will find singing. When America quit singing the enemy won a great victory. Get into the habit of singing to yourself. Make up love songs to the Lord or sing a tune to the words of a Psalm. There will be singing and rejoicing in heaven so you might as well get into practice.

3.   <u>Spiritual warfare is prayer.</u> What a comforting, confidence builder we have when we understand that we can stay in God's fortified place of prayer.

"Let us therefore come boldly to the throne of grace, that we may obtain mercy and find grace to help in time of need." Hebrews 4:16

To come boldly literally means "without reservation, with frankness, with full and open speech". <u>Always run to God and never away from Him.</u> He knows you better than you know yourself and He understands where you are in your walk of faith. Best of all, He is always there for you. (See Chapter 7)

Kingdom Warfare

The Kingdom of God (that you are now a citizen of if you have by faith received Jesus Christ as your Savior), is like a battlefield. There are two well-trained, well-equipped, opposing forces facing off in a daily, life or death struggle.

Paul compared it with a wrestling match where each fighter tries to hold the other down for the count. In ancient days it has been said the loser of a wrestling match had his eyes gouged out. This picture is meant to remind you our warfare is often hand to hand combat. We are at war now and war is not kiddies play time.

> *"For we do not wrestle against flesh and blood, but against principalities, against powers, against the rulers of the darkness of this age, against spiritual hosts of wickedness in the heavenly places." Ephesians 6:12*

War in Heaven

In the beginning it was the heavenly hosts of good angels against those fallen angels that chose to follow the mighty Lucifer in the great rebellion. Lucifer is the personal name of the devil referring to Satan, the enemy of God, of man, and of good.

We know very little about the ancient history of the devil other than he was one of the exalted angelic beings who became proud and ambitious. (Isaiah 14: 12-14) His decision to overthrown God's throne and take God's place resulted in his being thrown out of Heaven, along with one-third of God's angels. In Luke 10:18, Jesus said, "I saw Satan fall like lightning from heaven." That day must have shook things up a bit, wouldn't you say?

Old Testament Saints

Throughout the Old Testament Satan's evil army fought to destroy God's people knowing his time was short--the coming Messiah had been promised and he knew first-hand God does what He says He will do. Satan would never forget his defeat in the Garden of Eden.

> *"So the Lord God said to the serpent: Because you have done this you are cursed more than all cattle, and more than every beast of the field; On your belly you shall go and you shall eat dust all the days of your life. and I will put enmity between you and the woman, and between your seed and her Seed. He shall bruise your head, and you shall bruise His heel." Genesis 3: 14,15*

The Messiah Jesus

When Jesus was born Satan was hard at work trying to destroy the Savior before He could fulfill His destiny--the redemptive work of the cross. After Jesus Christ's triumph over sin and evil powers was accomplished, Satan now focused his attention toward the people of God, the Church and Body of Jesus Christ.

Today you can clearly see Satan's influence in the world. His various titles reflect this evil work:

- accuser of the brethren (Revelation 12:10)
- ruler of this world (John 12:31)
- father of lies (John 8:44)
- angel of light (2 Corinthians 1:14)
- god of this age (2 Corinthians 4:4)
- your father the devil (John 8:44)
- prince of the power of the air (Ephesians 2:2)
- wicked one (I John 5:19)
- thief (John 10:10)

While it may be difficult to admit we have such an enemy, the Bible makes it plain that Satan exists and that his main work is to "steal, kill, and destroy" followers of Jesus Christ. One of the hardest things about recognizing the enemy is that his work is invisible works of darkness. This is what Jesus said:

> *"The thief does not come except to steal, and to kill, and to destroy. I have come that they may have life, and that they may have it more abundantly." John 10:10*

Victory has been declared. Jesus' death, burial and resurrection brings victory over sin, the Law, and death. Although Satan is a defeated enemy, he refuses to surrender. We are told in the Word that the ultimate overthrow of this enemy will come swiftly.

> *"And the God of peace will crush Satan under your feet shortly..." Romans 16:20*

> *"But thanks be to God, who gives us the victory through our Lord Jesus Christ." I Corinthians 15:57*

The Whole Armor

In the meantime, you have everything needed to have personal victory on a daily basis. Spiritual victory is something you enter into since Jesus has already won it for you on the cross.

Second only to the power of the blood, you have been provided a defensive barrier against the spiritual attacks of the enemy called the armor of God. Great is the protection and resources available to those who walk in obedient faith. This protection cannot be emphasized enough since spiritual warfare continues to be our daily experience.

> *"Finally, my brethren, be strong in the Lord and in the power of His might. Put on the whole armor of God, that you may be able to stand against the wiles of the devil." Ephesians 6: 10,11*

You must learn to deal with daily struggles by being "strong in the Lord and in the power of His might". If you do not have the strength of His abiding presence that comes from living in God's fortified place this command to put on the whole armor of God, will not mean much. To stand against the wiles or schemes of the devil, means you must hold off aggressively or hold your position against the well-planned, strategic battle-plan of the enemy. This is accomplished through prayer and praise, dressed for battle.

Have you ever asked yourself what is the armor of God? While the reference in Ephesians 6, is obvious, it is easy to miss the real meaning. Picture yourself dressed in the armor of God. What do you see? A belt, a breastplate, boots, a shield and helmet?

The armor is not that! As a Christian soldier:

You stand in (1) truth--openness, honesty, sincerity, truthfulness with no deceit or pretention.

You stand in (2) sanctifying righteousness produced by the Holy Spirit, which is integrity, moral rectitude and right standing with God.

You stand in (3) peace. You have peace with God through the blood of Jesus and your life is a message of peace to a world in turmoil.

You stand in (4) faith. This is a present faith in Jesus for daily victory over sin and temptation.

You stand in a present-day (5) salvation, being saved daily from the power of sin.

You stand on the (6) Word of God, which is your weapon of choice against the enemy.

You stand watch in unceasing prayer. (Ephesians 6:18)

Chapter Nine

The Sphere of God

If you read either of my first two books, "Surrounded", or "Believe Beyond Basics", you will recall the supernatural encounter I had that was literally my "burning bush" experience. I was awakened with these words: "Draw a circle and a dot!" I love how my Heavenly Father speaks to me in such simple, childlike one-liners that I can understand. I immediately jumped up, grabbed a pad and pencil and drew a large circle. As I was putting a dot in the center of the circle revelation came into my mind that the dot was me. I am completely surrounded by God the Father, God the Son, and God the Holy Spirit. I thought, no matter which way I turn, I'm covered. To use an old adage, how cool is that!

The next morning there it was--my circle and dot. I shared what I had learned with my husband, but no one else. It was clear to me this was beyond anything I could ask or think. I didn't know what it meant, but I did understand two things: I am surrounded by Almighty God and I have His love, His protection, and His provision. This was crystal clear. For my Heavenly Father to go to such lengths to help me grasp His love is simply overwhelming and I never tire of sharing this divine encounter.

The following Sunday we were in church listening to a good sermon when the pastor said, "In closing, I just want to say, it's a circle and a dot! Turn to Titus 2:14." Russ and I jumped about a foot off the pew and quickly began turning pages in our bibles. Titus is one of the little books that tries to hide from you if you're in a hurry to find it. Many people go immediately to the front of the Bible to the list of books, which I highly recommend, or you may find it by going over in your mind, the Books of the Bible Song, as my son recently reminded me... "Titus and Philemon". This is called a "rabbit trail", in case you didn't notice. Now back to my story..

"(Jesus Christ) Who gave Himself for us, that He might redeem us from every lawless deed and purify for Himself His own special (peculiar) people, zealous for good works."
Titus 2:14

Pastor began briefly instructing on the word "peculiar", or "special". Low and behold, this word is pictured by a dot within a circle!

I have learned that every true revelation from God will always have its foundation in the Word of God. This was my confirmation.

In the weeks following the Holy Spirit began instructing me what God wanted me to do with this revelation of the circle and dot. For several years I served with an international mission organization as missionary to elementary school- age children before launching out into Gloria Russell Children's Ministry. During that same time the U.S. Supreme Court ruled in favor of Christian organizations having equal-access into public schools for after-school Bible clubs. G.R.C.M. was ready to begin Circle Club. This has a lot to do with Titus 2:14, and God setting us apart for Himself, zealous for good works. To God be the glory! The first year we had twelve Circle Clubs, with approximately forty volunteer workers. Every year since we have taught over 500 children every week for one hour after school.

Now what does this have to do with the sphere of God? Today, I picked up a book published in 1973, written by Kenneth Wuest, who was a teacher with Moody Bible Institute Radio out of Chicago. The first chapter was titled, The Peculiar People of God. He wrote:

"The word "peculiar" is found in Titus 2:14. Christians are the peculiar people of God. We use the word sometimes when we speak of something odd or strange. But that is not its use here. The word is translated from a Greek word which is made up of two words, one which means "around," as a circle, and the other which means "to be." It can be charted by a dot within a circle...As the circle is around the dot, so God is around each one of His saints. The circle monopolizes the dot, has the dot all to itself. So God has His own all to Himself. They are His own private unique possession. He has reserved them for Himself."

I get it! This is way beyond cool. When you are living in God's fortified place you are protected. Nothing can harm you in that powerful sphere of God. To get to you, the dot, nothing can reach you without going through the circle. You are a peculiar, special child of God, much loved, having His complete provision for all your needs, and always protected through the trials of this life.

There's much to discover about being one of God's own highly favored people. I have started drawing a small circle and dot in my Bible beside verses that picture the idea of God's protective circle. Let's look at several:

- *"Consecrate yourselves therefore, and be holy, for I am the Lord your God. And you shall keep My statutes and perform them. I am the Lord who sanctifies you." Leviticus 20: 7,8*

This command is not a suggestion or an option if you are a follower of Jesus Christ. God promises to set you apart unto Himself. Consecrate, holy, and sanctifies, all three express the concept of the sphere of God.

- *"The beloved of the Lord shall dwell in safety by Him, Who shelters him all the daylong..." Deuteronomy 33:12*

Safety in this verse speaks of security, peace, the state of confidence that belongs to those who trust and rely on the Lord in the shelter of His care.

- *"The eternal God is your refuge, and underneath are the everlasting arms..." Deuteronomy 33:27a*

The everlasting arms of our God are never exhausted. His protection is a promise He makes to every obedient child of God.

- *"As for God His way is perfect. The word of the Lord is proven. He is a shield to all who trust in Him." 2 Samuel 22:31*

This is more evidence of God's protective circle that surrounds His children.

- *"But know that the Lord has set apart for Himself him who is godly. The Lord will hear when I call to Him." Psalm 4:3*

In God's circle is a fortified place where prayer is answered when you call on your Heavenly Father. As a child of God you have His undivided attention.

- *"For You O Lord will bless the righteous. With favor You will surround him as with a shield." Psalm 5:12*

The gift of God's favor means He is pleased with or favorable toward something. In this case, you are the favored. God is pleased with you and His grace is available to accomplish things otherwise impossible.

- *"May the Lord answer you in the day of trouble. May the Name of the God of Jacob defend you. May He send you help from the sanctuary and strengthen you out of Zion." Psalm 20:1,2*

In the days following the circle and dot encounter I continued to receive more revelation. In these verses we find our God is always ready to help those He loves. He is a faithful God who defends you; He provides help and strength by His great power.

My most recent discovery is from Galatians 5:16.

- *"I say then: Walk in the Spirit, and you shall not fulfill the lust of the flesh."*

This is one of the commands requiring immediate and constant obedience--continuous action. It is saying, walk (and keep on walking). Believers are to continually live in complete dependence on the Holy Spirit and His empowering energy.

The big surprise is the word, "Spirit," referring to the Holy Spirit. This word is also pictured as a dot within a circle. The dot is encircled within a circle. The word is saying, "Be constantly conducting yourself in the sphere of the Spirit." It's a circle and a dot!

What about Ephesians 1:6?

- *"To the praise of the glory of His grace, by which He made us accepted in the Beloved."*

In one of my study Bibles the footnote for this verse says, "In Christ is a recurring term designating the sphere in which all salvation is realized and the realm in which

God's Kingdom purposes are fulfilled--in the circle of the King's (Christ's) reign.

Wuest says of this verse, "The words in the Beloved, are locative of sphere. That is, God the Father freely bestowed on us the grace which saved us, and did so in the sphere of the Lord Jesus, His Person and His work on the cross." It's a circle and a dot!

How can we possibly grasp the love and protection our great, awesome God has for us, His children? He knew I would not know the Greek and Hebrew language of the original Scriptures, nor would I understand "Present Imperative" (continuous action), so the Holy Spirit summed it up for me (and you) by simply saying, **"It's a circle and a dot!"**

Chapter Ten

For The Glory Of God

"...But the Lord will be with you an everlasting light, and your God your glory.." Isaiah 60:19b

You were created for God's glory. Yes? But what does that really mean?

The Hebrew word for glory means, "heavy or weighty", and refers to the heavy, substantive, weightiness of God's Presence. It is a quality of God's character that emphasizes His exceeding greatness and authority.

Several years ago the Lord spoke these words into my spirit. "When I come in My glory I bring the full weight of all my Names." I've had lots of time to study and pray over this word and I'm beginning to get a glimmer of just how huge the reality of the presence of God actually is.

"But we all, with unveiled face, beholding as in a mirror the glory of the Lord, are being transformed into the same image from glory to glory, just as by the Spirit of the Lord." 2 Corinthians 3:18

We were created for His glory. Christ shares His divine glory with His followers. In the face of Jesus, we see the glory of God. His glory is brightly reflected in our faces like in a mirror, because Jesus has removed the veil of sin from us. As you grow in the grace and knowledge of our Lord, you are being transformed into His image and will be presented faultless before the Father. Nothing of flesh lives here.

David's Desire

"As the deer pants for the water brooks, so pants my soul for You, O God. My soul thirsts for God, for the living God. When shall I come and appear before God?" Psalm 42:1,2

The Psalms of David are filled with the heart-cry of a man seeking a deep, personal relationship with the Lord Himself. David had come to understand that he cannot find the satisfaction and fulfillment he deeply desires in any other. He desires to know the Lord, not simply as his Savior, or even as King of Kings who can do great things for him. David's desire was to know the Lord as a Person with whom he can share times of intimate fellowship.

When David fell into sin, losing the joy of his salvation, he knew where to turn--back to his God. He repented before the Lord, receiving forgiveness and freedom from guilt and condemnation.

"I acknowledged my sin to You, and my iniquity I have not hidden. I said, 'I will

confess my transgressions to the Lord', and You forgave me the iniquity of my sin...You are my hiding place; You shall preserve me from trouble; You shall surround me with songs of deliverance." Psalm 32: 5, 7

David experienced a new level of intimacy with the Lord when he turned to Him with all his heart. The Spirit of God began to share deep, personal promises to encourage and uplift David's spirit.

"I will instruct you and teach you in the way you should go; I will guide you with My eye. Do not be like the horse or like the mule, which have no understanding, which must be harnessed with bit and bridle, else they will not come near you. Many sorrows shall be to the wicked; but he who trusts in the Lord, mercy shall surround him." Psalm 32:8-10

Today, you and I need the same clarity of Spirit-led protection and guidance that David experienced. Wouldn't you like to have a face-to-face encounter with the living God, where you come face-to-face with the goodness and glory of God? That is also the desire of God's heart. He is always calling us higher and deeper into Him where He reveals different aspects of His glory to us so we can experience Him in a greater way in our fortified place.

Moses' Desire

> *"And he [Moses] said, 'Please show me Your glory'." Exodus 33:18*

This account of Moses was after he had experienced many miraculous events, including the burning bush experience, the plagues in Egypt, parting of the Red Sea, the presence of the Lord in a cloud by day and fire by night, and the Lord speaking to him face to face as a man speaks to his friend.

When Moses spoke to the Lord face to face as a man speaks to his friend, his request was specific. He asked for the Lord to show him His glory. Moses was not asking to see another miracle or some physical blessing. He wanted to know God in all His glory (literally "weight"), meaning Moses wanted to have a deeper understanding and a more intimate relationship with God than he had experienced before. He wanted to know who God is--the Person He really is as he said in Exodus 33:13.

> *"...show me now Your way, that I may know You and that I may find grace in Your sight..."*

The Lord was pleased with Moses' desire to know Him more and more. He gave Moses a great and precious promise.

> *"And He said, "My Presence will go with you, and I will give you rest." Exodus 33:14*

The Lord told Moses that he had found grace in His sight. The meaning of grace in this scripture means unmerited favor. Moses had favor with God so he could ask for the desire of his heart, which was more than the Lord's Presence--more than His miracles--more than His favor. Moses wanted more of God Himself.

The Lord responded to Moses by telling him how he could experience a lasting satisfaction of and more intimate knowledge of God.

"I will make all My goodness pass before you and I will proclaim the name of the Lord before you..." Exodus 33:19

I didn't understand the significance nor the connection between God's goodness and His name until the Holy Spirit reminded me of what God spoke into my spirit during a previous study on the names of God and the characteristics associated with His name. "When I come in My glory I bring the full weight of all My names."

The Lord hid Moses in the cleft of the rock and manifested His glory in the weighty presence of his Name.

Glory Revealed

The glory of God has already been given to the Church through Christ, the risen Lord. When God comes in His glory He will fill you with the fullness of His glorious presence and you will begin to understand who He is and who you are in Him. God wants to bring you into a higher place of understanding where you are fully aware that the God of glory lives inside of you. The Holy Spirit, who was also in Jesus has come to live and abide in every believer. You are the temple of the Holy Spirit, chosen by God to bear His image and likeness to a world desperately in need of a manifestation of the glory of God. Today, you experience the goodness of God and know Him more intimately through the work of the Holy Spirit as He reveals more of Jesus, Who came to reveal all the goodness of Almighty God.

> *"For I consider that the sufferings of this present time are not worthy to be compared with the glory which shall be revealed in us. For the earnest expectation of the creation eagerly waits for the revealing of the sons of God." Romans 8: 18, 19*

This means that you have the awesome privilege and responsibility to carry the weighty presence of God's glory into every area of life. As the glorious weight of His presence intensifies within you and around you, the Lord will come in the power of all His Names. These are the ways you can know Him more.

GOOD SHEPHERD

> *"I am the good Shepherd. The good shepherd gives His life for the sheep." John 10:11*

Jesus reveals to us Jehovah Rohi--the Lord my Shepherd. Everything a shepherd could possibly be to his sheep, Jesus is to us. Psalm 23, tells about our wonderful Shepherd providing our every need so we want for nothing.

PEACE

"Peace I leave with you. My peace I give to you..." John 1:27

In this scripture Jesus reveals to us Jehovah-Shalom--the Lord is peace. His presence gives you perfect peace. In a world filled with chaos and confusion you can run into His arms, always outstretched to give you His protection and precious peace.

THE DOOR

"I am the door: by Me if any man enter in, he shall be saved..." John 10:9a

Jesus is "Thura"--the Door, a living door. All who enter in through Him find peace and safety and refuge from life's trials and burdens.

We could consider other names connected with Jesus.

RIGHTEOUSNESS

"...This is His name whereby He shall be called, The Lord Our Righteousness." Jeremiah 23:6

Jehovah Tsidkenu describes God who is perfectly righteous. Right standing with God comes through faith in Jesus alone.

> *"...in Christ Jesus, who became for us wisdom from God, and righteousness and sanctification and redemption that as it is written, He who glories let him glory in the Lord." I Corinthians 1:30,31*

Jesus took all our sin to the cross paying the payment in full with His precious blood so you and I can "become the righteousness of God in Him." (2 Corinthians 5:21)

SANCTIFIER"

> *"And for their sakes I sanctify Myself, that they also may be sanctified by the truth." John 17:1*

Jehovah M'Kaddesh is the Lord Who Sanctifies. Jesus came to restore believers ruined by sin to a position of holiness or cleansing from the guilt and power of sin. He sets us apart from the world unto Himself. (Titus 2:14)

It's time for God's glory to be seen-- in you! This is the Light that dispels darkness. Jesus Himself declared, "I am the Light of the world." Then again He said, "You are the light of the world." The closer you get into the presence of the Lord, and begin to stay there, the more of His glory will be in you and upon you. This weighty presence of the Lord is in the fortified place and you are invited to stake your claim to that place as your permanent dwelling.

Paul's Assignment

"That we who first trusted in Christ should be to the praise of His glory." Ephesians 1:12

The book of Ephesians was written to all believers that we might understand the wealth of God's investment in each of us. He carefully lays out the case for holy living. We are to become experientially what God made us to be positionally. All that we have received in Christ through salvation was for the glory of God, and was paid for by the blood of Jesus.

"For you were bought with a price, therefore glorify God in your body and in your spirit, which are God's." 1 Corinthians 6:20

We need a deeper understanding of God's glory. The glory brightens dark places. God's glory overpowers darkness and darkness cannot hide. As you live in obedient faith and submission to God's leading and His glorious presence begins to manifest in your life you become a praise to Him bringing glory to His Name.

"Let your light so shine before men that they may see your good works and glorify your Father in heaven." Matthew 5:16

Our daily prayer should be an expression of the significance of His glory and of our desire to be a praise of His glory. Pray with me:

Lord, be glorified in my life...be glorified in my home...
be glorified in my family...be glorified in my work...be
glorified in my church. Let your glory be seen in me.

Pathway to Glory

Glory is not the easiest concept to understand.
You can, however, understand that if you live your life
according to God's Word, God's Ways, and God's Will,
you bring Him glory. This is the path to glory you need
to follow. The results will be to see His glory.

You and I live in the greatest transition of our lifetime.
While the world seems to grow darker God's people walk
in the Light. One of the great characteristics of this hour
is that our ability to see into the supernatural things of
God is being enhanced and our understanding is being
enlightened by the Holy Spirit at work in us. This is a time
of the fulfillment of Paul's prayer in Ephesians 1: 18,19.

> *"By having the eyes of your heart flooded with
> light, so that you can know and understand the
> hope to which He has called you, and how rich
> is His glorious inheritance in the saints (His
> set-apart ones), And [so that you can know
> and understand] what is the immeasurable
> and unlimited and surpassing greatness
> of His power in and for us who believe, as
> demonstrated in the working of His mighty
> strength." Ephesians 1: 18,19 Ampli.*

As you submit to the work of the indwelling Holy Spirit of God, He makes known the divine secrets of God's Word, God's ways, and God's will and the end result will be that He receives the glory due His name.

<u>Digest God's Word</u> -- God wants to open the eyes of your understanding into the way His Word works in your life. Ephesians 1: 18,19 is a great place to begin:

- The hope of His calling -- This hope is the confident, earnest, expectation of the goodness of God and His faithfulness to fulfill all His plans and promises.

- The riches of His inheritance in the saints -- This is a revelation of just how precious you are to God.

- The exceeding greatness of His power -- The Holy Spirit is the power-pack of God. His power is beyond measure, more than enough, super-abounding power at work in your life today. We're talking about God's power here.

<u>Learn God's Ways</u>

"...I will instruct you and teach you in the way you should go; I will guide you with My eye."
Psalm 32:76

This scripture is God's response to obedient faith. David messed up. A man after God's own heart, sinned against God. When he acknowledged his sin and confessed to God, he was forgiven and received this great and precious promise of God's instruction and guidance found in Psalm 32.

Today you and I can learn from this Word. The Holy Spirit has been sent. He lives inside every true believer to instruct and teach the ways of our God.

Walk in God's will-- God's will is how you are to live and conduct yourself--what you think, what you say, and what you do. God's plan is that you become transformed into the image of His Son.

> *"In Him also we have obtained an inheritance, being predestined according to the purpose of Him who works all things according to the counsel of His will that we who first trusted in Christ should be to the praise of His glory."*
> *Ephesians 1: 11,12*

God has a perfect will for your life. This is how you are to walk, how you are to live, and conduct yourself; what you are to think, what you are to say, and what you do. Does your life demonstrate the will of God or self-will? (John 7: 16,17)

I like to think of "the counsel of His will", being decided around a long mahogany table in the counsel room of God before creation, as the Father, His Son, and the mighty Holy Spirit sat "at counsel" making plans according to His "good pleasure". Just as you were in Him, on the cross, you were also on His mind as God planned out the centuries that lay before Him. He knows every one of His own and His will for your life is perfect, tailor-made just for you.

You are to be careful how you live each day. God cares. He sees all, hears all, and knows all. His will is always what is best in every circumstance--at all times. I love this thought from Proverbs 18. The word safe implies lifted up out of reach. When you live according to God's will you are lifted high above the dangers of the world. What a promise!

"The name of the Lord is a strong tower. The righteous run to it and are safe." Proverbs 18:10

Chapter Eleven

The Security of Love

To wake up every morning with an awareness of being in your fortified place, surrounded by God's covenant circle of love is your most precious gift as a follower of Jesus Christ. His presence brings the perfect peace and security you long for and seek most of your life.

Paul's Prayer

Ephesians 3:14-20, gives a great prayer that addresses this heart-felt need--to know the love of Christ. The Apostle prays for the Holy Spirit's power to fill every believer with the strength of Christ's presence and love.

> *"For this reason I bow my knees to the Father of our Lord Jesus Christ, from whom the whole family in heaven and earth is named, that he would grant you, according to the riches of His glory, to be strengthened with might through His Spirit in the inner man, that Christ may dwell in your hearts through faith, that you, being rooted and grounded in love, may*

Be able to comprehend with all the saints what is the width and length and depth and height--to know the love of Christ which passes knowledge, that you may be filled with all the fullness of God." Ephesians 3:14-19

Have you ever asked yourself why it is so difficult to grasp or comprehend the "extravagant dimensions" of the love shown to us by Jesus Christ? If Paul prayed this prayer in Ephesians 3, then so can you.

Nicodemus

Jesus came into the world to show us the Father and His great love for mankind. One night a very influential and respected member of the Sanhedrin came to see Jesus. He was a Pharisee, trained in Jewish law and theology and a teacher, but he failed to understand the love of God as shown in the Person of Jesus Christ. Nicodemus had one thing in his favor. He was a seeker. He wanted to know if Jesus was the Messiah, the Promised One he had been looking for, so he came to see Jesus, personally.

After explaining to Nicodemus that he needed to be born again, Jesus gave the most powerful invitation in all of scripture.

"For God so loved the world that He gave His only begotten Son that whoever believes in Him should not perish but have everlasting life." John 3:16

The word Jesus used for love is agape, meaning a love produced in the heart of a yielded believer by the Holy Spirit, called out of one's heart by the preciousness of the one loved, compelling one to sacrifice one's self for the one loved. <u>Read that again</u>!

Peter's Example

After the resurrection, Jesus appeared to those who followed Him. The 3rd time was on the seashore where He prepared breakfast for the disciples who had been out fishing all night. After they had eaten Jesus spoke personally with Peter, asking,

> *"...Simon, son of Jonah, do you love Me more than these?" John 21:15-17*

The word Jesus used here for love is agape. Peter couldn't say that he loved Jesus that much so he answered, "Yes, Lord, You know I have affection for you."

A second time Jesus asked the same question and Peter's response was the same. Then a third time Jesus said,

> *"...Simon, son of Jonah, do you have affection for Me?"*

Peter was grieved that Jesus would ask three times, but he could not commit to agape love so soon after he had denied even knowing Jesus. The betrayal was too fresh--too raw. How could he say I love you with a sacrificial love when he had failed so miserably?

Oh, what love and compassion we find in Jesus. He accepted Peter where he was knowing change was coming. Peter would soon understand agape love. The change would begin when the Holy Spirit came in power on the Day of Pentecost. We know this is true because later, in his writings Peter speaks of agape love nine times.

You can't miss the important role the Holy Spirit has in revealing God's love for you. When you give the Holy Spirit His proper place in your life, He turns the spotlight on Jesus and the unconditional love He has for us.

> *"...the love of God has been poured out in our hearts by the Holy Spirit who was given to us."*
> *Romans 5:5*

Feelings vs. Faith

Perhaps, like me, you have said, "I don't feel loved." Guess what? You don't have to feel anything. However, you do have to believe. Yes, that again. You believe in Jesus as Savior. Now believe what God's Word says about love. Put your faith in solid evidence rather than passing emotions. This is what God says:

> *"...Yes, I have loved you with an everlasting love. Therefore with loving kindness I have drawn you." Jeremiah 31:3*

Agape Love

There's much for us to learn about God's kind of love found in the word "agape".

- It is a love called out of one's heart by the preciousness of the one loved, compelling one to sacrifice one's self for the one loved.

- It is an undefeatable benevolence and unconquerable goodwill that always seeks the highest good of the other person, no matter what he does.

- It is a self-giving love that gives freely without asking anything in return. (Hosea14:4)

- It does not consider the worth of its object.

- It is love by choice rather than chance.

- It compels us to live our life for Jesus.

- It is an attribute of God as well as an essential part of His nature. (I John 4:8,16)

- It is everlasting. (Jeremiah 31:3)

- It shows to others you are a Christian. (John 13:34,35)

- It never fails but always flourishes. (I Corinthians 13:8)

The closest picture we have of agape love in human relationships is a mother's love for her child. However, love found its perfect expression in Jesus.

"But God demonstrates His own love toward us in that while we were still sinners, Christ died for us." Romans 5:8

"By this we know love, because He laid down His life for us..." I John 3:16a

Walk In Love

"And walk in love, as Christ also has loved us and given Himself for us..." Ephesians 5:2a

"Walk" means to live, conduct one's self, one's behavior. Many of us teethed on John 3:16 and "Jesus Love Me". You may easily repeat the words but the evidence may not be there to prove the Word is actually working in your life.

Today, rejoice that you belong to our Father God and that you live in the circle of His love. Check your "Love-o-Meter" often to make sure your love-life is what it should be. Here are several points to look for:

"He who does not love does not know God, for God is love." I John 4:8

- Love for fellow believers. (I Jn. 3:14, 4:7,21; John 15:12; Hebrews 13:1)

- Obey Jesus' commandments. (John 14:15,21; 15:10)

- Hatred for evil. (I John 2:15)

- Habitual sin. (I John 3:9)

- Love of money (I Timothy 6:10)

- Love for your spouse. (Titus 2:4; Ephesians 5:25)

<u>When love becomes the deciding factor in your choices and the motivating power of your actions you will be walking in love.</u>

Chapter Twelve

Understanding God's Covenant of Protection

A covenant in the Biblical sense is a permanent arrangement between two people that covers each one's total being--all aspects of each one's life.

God's covenant with His people involves a holy, all-knowing, and all powerful God entering into covenant with man who is weak, sinful, imperfect, and completely unable to fulfill his side.

From the Garden of Eden to the throne room in Heaven, the blood sacrifice pictures cleansing, forgiveness, and redemption. All through the old covenant, a blood sacrifice was required. The slain, innocent animal was a little picture of the ultimate sacrifice for sin when the blood of the sinless Lamb, Jesus Christ was shed for all mankind.

Jeremiah the prophet wrote about the new covenant God would make with mankind based on the death and resurrection of Christ. This covenant is a better covenant made with better promises and does not depend on man's ability to keep the law. (Hebrews 8:6)

"Behold, the days are coming, says the Lord, when I will make a new covenant with the house of Israel and with the house of Judah-- not according to the covenant that I made with their fathers...But this is the covenant that I will make with the house of Israel after those days, says the Lord: I will put My law in their minds, and write it on their hearts, and I will be their God, and they shall be My people."
Jeremiah 31:31-33

In the new covenant God would accomplish for his people what the old covenant failed to do. It is the blood of Christ that satisfied the just demands of God's holy law which decreed, "The wages of sin is death."

"In Him we have redemption through His blood, the forgiveness of sins, according to the riches of His grace..." Ephesians 1:7

God's Family Plan

God's heart has always been to establish relationship with mankind. Sin separated man from God. It is only through the shed blood of Christ that payment for all sins, past and present, has been accomplished. Through the new covenant sacrifice of Christ's blood we are brought into the covenants of promise. Through faith in the blood of Christ mankind is justified in God's eyes and a right relationship can be established with a holy God.

"For He made Him who knew no sin to be sin for us, that we might become the righteousness of God in Him." 2 Corinthians 5:21

Jesus used the occasion of the Passover meal to inaugurate this new covenant. That night He transformed the meaning of the elements of this meal by declaring the bread now represented His body which would be given, and the cup His blood, which would be shed for the forgiveness of sins.

"And He said to them, 'This is My blood of the new covenant, which is shed for many." Mark 14:24

Power of Covenant

You and I are in a covenant relationship with God. Everything we have and everything we are flow from that covenant relationship. Through our covenant position with God, we stand clean and blameless before Him through the blood of Jesus. Our victory has always been and will always be in Jesus.

"But thanks be to God, who gives us the victory through our Lord Jesus Christ." I Corinthians 15:57

We can understand God's plan for our lives. Our place in Christ gives confidence and courage to go after everything God has for us.

"Therefore do not cast away your confidence, which has great reward." Hebrews 10:35

Through prayer we have access to the throne room and into the very Presence of God and you cannot outstay your welcome. This verse suggests you can stay there.

"Let us therefore come boldly to the throne of grace, that we may obtain mercy and find grace to help in time of need." Hebrews 4:16

Keeping Covenant

Once you understand covenant is relationship with the Lord you must go to war against covenant breaking. God keeps covenant, so you must choose to keep covenant with the understanding this is possible because the Holy Spirit who lives in you has sealed your covenant with God and God's covenant seal cannot be broken.

"In Him you also trusted, after you heard the word of truth, the gospel of your salvation in whom also, having believed you were sealed with the Holy Spirit of promise...Who is the guarantee of our inheritance..." Ephesians 1:13,14a

Advance In Victory

It is critical that we continue to learn how to outwit the enemy in these last days. We all agree he can come at us at times and catch us completely off guard. Some believe he saved his most powerful, effective weapons for today. Past generations of believers would argue this point.

David had a covenant with God. The principals in Psalm 89, show how this covenant with God positions you to overcome the schemes of the enemy. You need to apply these in your war against satan today.

1. A New Anointing

"J have found my servant David, with My holy oil J have anointed him." Psalm 89:20

To anoint means to consecrate, or make sacred, or to formally choose for a sacred task. Anointing carries with it the authority necessary to do the job. As believers, our covenant with God positions you to receive the anointing and authority we need to outwit the enemy.

2. A New Strength

Psalm 89:21 "With whom My hand shall be established, also My arm shall strengthen him." Jsaiah 52:1 "Awake, awake! Put on your strength..."

Strength is (a)to have power, vigor, might, energy and fervency. (b) to have power by reason of influence, authority or resources. (c) to have power to withstand an attack.

Strength is something that you actually have to put on. We need to regularly inspect our armor and make needed repairs in preparation for the next battle. This is an attitude check.

Gloria Russell

Your covenant with God positions you for strength over the enemy by the very influence, authority, and resources He makes available to you.

3. A Partner- In- Battle

Psalm 89:23 "I will beat down his foes before his face, and plague those who hate him."

Because you are in covenant with the Lord, He overthrows the power of the enemy on your behalf. God fights for you.

Isaiah 59:19b "When the enemy comes in like a flood, the Spirit of the Lord will lift up a standard against him."

The lifting or setting up of a standard implies a peculiar presence, protection and aid in leading and directing God's people to do His will. Your covenant positions you under God's powerful standard.

4. New Revelation

Revelation means receiving knowledge or understanding from the Holy Spirit that is beyond your natural ability to attain. You have the revelation needed to advance in victory through prayer. You have an open invitation into the throne room where you can seek the Lord for strategic warfare. Every battle is won in your fortified place of prayer.

Precious Promises of Protection

Those who choose to follow Jesus and to live in His fortified place of protection have been accepted by the Father and empowered by the Holy Spirit in a permanent covenant. It is a covenant of protection. We look to the Word of God for clearer understanding of God's covenant of protection and find the riches of His grace poured out in our hearts.

- God is our strength.

"The Lord is my Rock and my fortress, and my deliverer, my God, my strength, in whom I will trust--my shield and the horn of my salvation, my stronghold." Psalm 18:2

- God protects from evil.

"But the Lord is faithful, who will establish you and guard you from the evil one." 2 Thessalonians 3:3

- God protects when temptation comes.

"No temptation has overtaken you except such as is common to man; but God is faithful, who will not allow you to be tempted beyond what you are able, but with the temptation will also make the way of escape, that you may be able to bear it." 1 Corinthians 10:13

- God protects from the cares of life.

"...casting all your care upon Him, for He cares for you." 1 Peter 5:7

- God protects from danger.

"Surely He shall deliver you from the snare of the fowler and from the perilous pestilence. He shall cover you with His feathers, and under His wings you shall take refuge. His truth shall be your shield and buckler. You shall not be afraid." Psalm 91: 3-5a

- God protects from fear.

"Fear not, for I am with you. Be not dismayed I am your God. I will strengthen you, yes, I will help you. I will uphold you with My righteous right hand." Isaiah 41:10

- God's protection is powerful.

"And I give them eternal life and they shall never perish, neither shall anyone snatch them out of My hand." John 10:28

- God's protection is forever.

"As the mountains surround Jerusalem so the Lord surrounds His people from this time forth and forever." Psalm 125:2

Chapter Thirteen

Name of the Lord

One of the most dynamic ways that God reveals Himself to us is through His name. There are hundreds of names in the Bible for our God. All are there to give us a deep appreciation of who He is and the many ways He protects and provides for His own. God relates to His people by His name. We need a fuller understanding of His precious name.

The "Name of the Lord" means all which the Lord Jesus is in His Person and work.

His name is above every name.

> *"Therefore God also has highly exalted Him and given Him the name which is above every name that at the name of Jesus every knee should bow...and that every tongue should confess that Jesus Christ is Lord, to the glory of God the Father." Philippians 2: 9a,10*

There's protection in His name.

> *"The name of the Lord is a strong tower. The righteous run to it and are safe." Proverbs 18:10*

This scripture says His name protects us not only by strength, but by height. The word safe as used here implies, "lifted out of reach, secure, set on high." Picture a walled fortress set high on a hill. This is your fortified place where you find help for every need.

There's joy in His name.

> *"For our heart shall rejoice in Him, because we have trusted in His holy name." Psalm 33:21*

Getting to know the Lord by personal experience brings great joy into your life. The Word also tells us the joy of the Lord is our strength. Praise and worship is an automatic response. One of the chorus' we sing has these words: Great is the Lord, and greatly to be praised. Every revelation you receive from the Holy Spirit about our God should have this affect--drawing you into His presence with powerful praise and worship of His holy name. The Psalms of David are filled with such a response from a heart filled with awe and wonder at the work of God's hand.

His name defeats the enemy.

> *"You are my King, O God...Through You we will push down our enemies. Through Your name we will trample those who rise up against us." Psalm 44: 4,5*

Perhaps you, like myself, have had a hard time identifying our "enemies". I have been blessed with wonderful sisters and brothers in the Lord, and have had very few or no actual people I consider to be an enemy. This is certainly one of the spiritual blessings of belonging to the church of Jesus Christ. So who are the enemies that we must push down?

Well put that way, this is a no brainer. You will have no problem identifying this enemy of your soul. Satan has been hard at work trying to destroy you since the first day you accepted Jesus as your Savior from sin. You may have been hit really hard and are wondering how you can survive. You can and you will. Get into the armor God has provided and keep on standing against the enemy. (see Chapter 8)

His name is our help.

"Our help is in the name of the Lord Who made heaven and earth." Psalm 124:8

The name of the Lord is not a get out of jail free card. When you invoke His name it is with heart-attitude. You recognize Who He is and what He has done to save you. You don't even have to speak His name for God to hear you and to come to your rescue.

I have a personal testimony of just such a time. Early one morning I was at my desk and a rhema word came into my thoughts, which I wrote down before leaving the house for a morning of Christmas shopping.

"God is our refuge and strength. A very present help in trouble." Psalm 46:1

Coming home the car veered to the left, crossing the other lane hitting a huge tree before spiraling to the right into a culvert then bouncing into the air for a loop to loop several times before landing in a field.

As I flew through the air I called out to God, "Help!" My thought was, "God, there's only You. Whatever you decide is right." Later that day back home with no injuries and my family around me I remembered the verse written on my desk and asked my granddaughter to read it to everyone. Help is a word God responds to. Isn't it amazing that this little prayer, "Help!" has been used twice in my lifetime during major emergencies-- once when I was just a small child and then many, many years later. God is no respecter of persons. He is the Help of all ages--anyone or anywhere.

There's blessings in His name.

"So they shall put My name on the children... and I will bless them." Numbers 6:27

There's nothing magical in saying the name of Jesus. However, when you decide from the heart to lay hands on your child and dedicate that child to the Lord, God will honor this act of obedience. He will be with you as you make decisions concerning your child's upbringing and bless that child as only He can.

Chapter Fourteen

War Over Words

Why are words so toxic?

Man was created in the image of God. We have a spirit and soul and we live in a body. The spirit is that inner part where the Holy Spirit comes to live when one is born again.

The soul of man is made up of three parts: the mind, the emotions, and the will. What you see and hear directly affects the mind, what you are thinking about, thus causing the emotions to be stirred either in a positive way or negative. How one feels dictates to the will what you will do --your actions.

Consider the fact that this cause and affect started at birth. You can understand how all of life is guided by the power of words. Everything that has been programmed into your mind through sight and sound affects your morals, your work drive, your integrity, and your life investment. Where you are in life today is where you or someone else talked you into. Where you are today should reflect what God says about you.

The wise writer of Proverbs observed,

"As a man thinks in his heart, so is he."
Proverbs 23:7

Someone recently wrote: Any thought you have that doesn't inspire hope is under the influence of a lie. Why is this true? Hope is confident expectation of the goodness and faithfulness of God to fulfill His plans and promises. It's all about trust. As I have said many times, I trust You, Lord, is our most powerful declaration. Say it! Say it again!

Who's in control?

Ever since God first spoke to Adam and Eve, instructing them so they would know how to live abundant, happy lives, there has been a consistent battle over who will control the thought processes of the mind--man or God.

It is simply not true that you cannot help how you feel. Feelings are not spontaneous. They are created by what you put into your mind. What you see and hear affect your thoughts and emotions. To control how you feel you must first control your mind by monitoring and altering the words you speak.

Jesus was talking about this in this scripture:

"Let this mind be in you which was also in Christ Jesus." *Philippians 2:5*

How is this relevant to control of your mind? Exactly what was in the mind of Christ that you can appropriate today?

1.   He knew who He was--God with us.

2.   He served with humility--even to death.

For the sake of this study, my point is obvious. God says to let the same mind-set be in you that Jesus demonstrated. He walked and talked as God. Today, you and I are in Him. You must know who you are in Christ and be confident of this truth. Walk like you are in Christ. Talk like you are in Christ. Act like you are in Christ.

When John the Baptist sent his followers to ask Jesus if He was the promised One, Jesus said, "Tell John the blind see and the lame walk, lepers are cleansed and the deaf hear, the dead are raised up and the poor have the gospel preached to them." (Matthew 11:4,5)

Today, it is important to acknowledge who you are in Christ. You need to say what God says about you and not what you may feel or what someone else has said. God is asking you to believe He is who He says He is, believe you are who He says you are, and then live like you believe those things.

In order for the mind of Christ to become your reality, your mind needs to be renewed to the Word of God. This is to progressively become like Christ as the Holy Spirit does His transforming work in you through the Word.

*"And be renewed in the spirit of your mind."
Ephesians 4:23*

*"Be transformed by the renewing of your mind that
you may prove what is that good and acceptable
and perfect will of God." Romans 12:2*

Danger of Strongholds

A stronghold is a mind-set impregnated with
hopelessness that causes one to accept as unchangeable,
situations that you know are contrary to the will of God.

Strongholds have to go! Just think of the power a
stronghold can have to hinder your prayers from being
answered. Hopelessness is quite different from hope,
is it not? It is opposite of faith and without faith it is
impossible to please God.

As thoughts are changed about who you are in
Christ, you will speak life into your emotions. Get some
faith talk going. Shatter that stronghold to pieces. This
will set the course for what you do the rest of your life as
you live (and speak) according to God's will.

*"And we...are being transformed into His likeness
with ever-increasing glory, which comes from the
Lord who is the Spirit." 2 Corinthians 3:18 NIV*

When you begin to speak what God says instead
of personal opinion or man's ideas, this confession
becomes a springboard to life-change, thus demolishing
your old way of thinking and establishing a new way of

thinking about yourself, life, God, your family and your world. You may be asking how can this be done?

The first step is to stop confessing lies. When you say what God says (confession) you begin to think what God thinks (repentance) and God's power will turn your life around (glory).

What are some things you say or think about yourself on a regular basis that disagrees with God's Word?

I'm just an 'ole sinner saved by grace. No you're not! That's a lie. If you have received Jesus as Savior you are a saint saved by grace. There's a big difference between a sinner and a saint. (Romans 1:4)

I can't do anything right. Wrong! You can do all things through Christ who gives you strength. (Philippians 4:13)

I won't ever amount to anything. Another lie. "In Christ" you are a victorious over-comer. You are somebody--a King's kid. (I John 5:4)

I just can't make it! Yes you can. God will supply all your needs. (Philippians 4:19)

I'm just a big, fat failure. That's not what God says. You are His workmanship--His handiwork, created in Christ for good works. (Ephesians 2:10)

The devil keeps stopping me. You can stop him with your shield of obedient faith. Let your faith speak! (Ephesians 6:16)

<u>Nobody loves me.</u> What a lie! You are greatly loved by your Heavenly Father. (Ephesians 2:4)

<u>I've lost all hope.</u> Stop right there. Your Father is the God of hope and you abound in hope by the power of the Holy Spirit. (Romans 15:13)

<u>I don't feel saved</u>. Salvation is not based on feelings, but on truth. If you believe on the Lord Jesus you are saved through His blood. Ask God for assurance. (Ephesians 1:7)

<u>This world is going to hell in a hand basket.</u> Not so. Our Father in Heaven is a God of redemption. His plan is perfect, right on time, and will stay on track according to His perfect will.

<u>I don't think God hears my prayers</u>. Why not? God says He will answer every prayer you pray in faith according to His will. (see Chapter 7)

A New Vocabulary

Change is never easy. When it comes to long established habits many never change. As you grow in the grace and knowledge of our Lord Jesus a new vocabulary will emerge before you know it.

"I thank God always concerning you for the grace of God which was given to you by Christ Jesus that you were enriched in everything by Him in all utterance and all knowledge." I Corinthians 1: 4,5

To be enriched in all utterance is to have the ability to speak faith-filled words that build up rather than tear down, discourage, or destroy. James wrote about the untamable tongue.

"For we all stumble in many things. If anyone does not stumble in word, he is a perfect man, able also to bridle the whole body." James 3:2

Perfect as used here means mature. James goes on to teach that the tongue can produce good and evil, blessing and cursing. It is notoriously inconsistent and must be tamed. Jesus also taught about the tongue.

"But those things which proceed out of the mouth come from the heart, and they defile a man." Matthew 15:8

As your mind, emotions, and will are renewed by the Word of God, your words will be controlled by the Spirit rather than the flesh and new life will flow out of your mouth.

When God Speaks

God's Word created the whole world along with everything in it--including mankind. He spoke and it was.

"It is written, Man shall not live by bread alone, but by every word that proceeds from the mouth of God." Matthew 4:4

In this scripture, the use of "word" is rhema, rather than logos. I shared the difference in another chapter, however, it is worth repeating. This means the believer must live--have our very being nurtured by what God is saying today. Hearing what God is saying is our life-source, as bread is to the body. We were created to walk and talk with God.

Recently, I was having a bad week. A most hurtful circumstance arose, knocking me off my feet. I simply had no answer and could not decide what I was to do. Every solution I came up with seemed to have an unthinkable consequence that had the potential for creating even more pain.

On Sunday morning, I was thanking God that He cared when a powerful, well-known scripture came flowing into my mind. "Casting all your care upon Him, for He cares for you." I Peter 5:7.

Even as I write this I am in awe at the power of this word. It changes everything. I have not been very successful in "casting all my care" this week, but the reminder of my Father's loving care and the absolute fact that He is more than able to take care of my little cares has lifted a great burden, even in the face of an unresolved situation. God is talking all the time. The words that "proceed from the mouth of God", will be exactly what you need for today. Be somewhere listening!

When Satan Speaks

Yes, the devil talks! Never allow the enemy to speak his deceptive lies into your spirit. They are deadly to your spiritual well-being. Remember what happened to Eve. Who would think she could be deceived into believing the Lord lied to her and Adam. What happened? For one thing the enemy was far more powerful than she was and he was a much more experienced foe. He thought he had the perfect set-up to trap her into agreeing with him. The fall was great, but God's redemptive plan of restoration was greater, and something satan knew nothing of.

Satan will always try to work his web of lies into something you will agree with. He knows you far more than you would like to think. Don't dialog with him and don't come into agreement with his condemning words by repeating them. Your sins were blotted out once and for all. Defeat the enemy by the overcoming power of the "blood of the Lamb", and declare your abiding faith in the accomplished work of the Cross. In this way you share in Christ's victory.

When a Believer Speaks

I'm sure you've been around individuals who by their words create an atmosphere of negative thoughts and feelings. When you get away from them you feel a great sense of relief. No one wants to be remembered in this way, however, sometimes the best of us have allowed our mind to slide right into an almost uncontrollable dark, negative side. I have been guilty of this far too many times and each time with regret I think, "I wish I had not said that", or "Where in the world did that come from?"

How can you avoid such days?

- Guard your heart! Focus! What you say often directs your next step. This can be deadly! It's like walking through a mind-field. When you are in a weak moment be very cautious. You must find your strength in Him. The Word of God speaks volumes on this subject.

"Guard the door of your mouth..." Micah 7:5

- Say something good! This is where the rubber hits the road, so to speak. Your next thought and spoken word is critical. If you simply cannot think of something good to say, go to the "good book", as the old folk used to say. Your Bible has the words God wants to hear. The Psalmist spoke powerful, life producing words. Notice in this verse his decision to say it. Use your voice for positive praise to God and see what the power of your words can do.

"I will say of the Lord, He is my refuge and my fortress, my God, in Him I will trust." Psalm 91:2

Chapter Fifteen

Borders and Boundaries

Some people say walls divide us -- others believe walls protect us. Both concepts are found in the Word of God.

The Boundary of Personal Gifts and Callings

Each of us has our assigned place and specific purpose to advance God's kingdom within our boundaries. In other words you should function within the boundaries of your individual gifts and calling. God's perfecting grace only works when you stay in your assigned place. It is only in God's perfect plan for your life that you will find fulfillment in life and rewards both here and in eternity.

Let's consider two important questions.

1. Who put you where you are?

2. Why are you there?

There can only be two answers: obedience or rebellion. Either God put you here or you put yourself here. It is of the utmost importance that you are in the place God has established and ordained. Ask the Lord to confirm your boundaries.

Paul wrote in Ephesians 1, that God chose you before the foundation of the world according to the good pleasure and counsel of His will. He alone has the perfect plan for your life. This includes where you live physically, who you marry, where you work, worship, and play. It is vital to your complete well-being that you are aligned with God's plan for your life--not to mention the safety of the people around you that your life touches and influences.

Within the sphere of God's sovereign plan for your life there are protective borders or boundaries. In that fortified place you have all grace, all spiritual blessings, all the precious promises, all power, and most important all the fullness of God's presence to live a life pleasing to God and to complete your personal assignment.

Let the Walls Come Down

"For He Himself is our peace, Who has made both one, and has broken down the middle wall of separation." Ephesians 2:14

Peace means two things. It is to bring together or unite something that is separated. It also means to bring an end to hostility.

Ephesians 2:14, is speaking of the Church of Jesus Christ. He said, "I will build My church." There are to be no walls of separation in His body. Jesus is the head and every believer has a part in His body: Jew and Gentile; slave and free men; male and female; young and old; rich and poor. Can you possibly imagine what this will look like when you stand with thousands upon thousands of individuals who by faith received Jesus Christ as Savior? They will come from every tongue, tribe, and nation. The invitation is open to whosoever will may come.

All through the Old Testament the designated places for worship had three distinct enclosed areas: the outer court, the Holy Place, and the Holy of Holies. A heavy, thick fabric was draped across the tabernacle to separate the Holy Place from the Holy of Holies where the ark of the covenant rested (representing the presence of God).

I read somewhere that God never did like that veil. When Jesus died on the cross at Calvary, God was the one who ripped the veil from top to bottom in the temple in such a way that it could never be rewoven. This curtain represented the dividing line or wall that separated Him from mankind. God never wants to be separated from His children. He does everything possible to destroy things that separate us from His presence.

Sin builds a wall of separation.

Moses was instructed to warn God's people about the danger of coming too close to Mt. Sinai, the mountain where he met with God. Boundaries had to be set to protect them from death when God came down in smoke and fire. They could not come near to God because God is holy and man is sinful. (Exodus 19)

God hates sin because sin separates. It took the ripping of the veil of His Son's flesh to pay the price for all sin. This was a terrible price to pay. In this payment, He "has broken down the middle wall of separation." It is the blood of Jesus that gives us access to God's throne-room today. In Christ Jesus, sinful man is made right (or holy) with God and the wall of separation is destroyed once and for all.

"For He made Him who knew no sin to be sin for us, that we might become the righteousness of God in Him." 2 Corinthians 5:21

Self-limitation builds a wall of separation.

Your humanness has certain boundaries. That's why you are limited in so many areas: your ability to love; your ability to forgive; your ability to have compassion, etc. Thank God the Holy Spirit lives in you to tear down walls of limitation and fill you with power to overcome these obstacles. Where once you were a slave to sin and the flesh, held in bondage by death and Satan, Jesus came to provide a way of escape from bondage, giving access into God's presence.

Build That Wall

God tears down walls that divide, and builds walls to protect. Within these protective walls is your fortified place where the enemy cannot touch you.

"For the scepter of wickedness shall not rest on the land allotted to the righteous..." Psalm 125:3

- Peace builds a wall of protection.

"For He has strengthened the bars of your gates...He makes peace in your borders..." Psalm 147: 11,13,14

God goes to great lengths to display His mercy in the life of a believer--especially one that is called to teach His Word.

- Prayer builds a wall of protection.

"J sought for a man among them who would make a wall, and stand in the gap before Me on behalf of the land that J should not destroy it, but J found no one..." Ezekiel 22:30

You can create a no-fly zone in prayer. As God's intercessor-on-assignment you can take your land, establish your borders, and re-dig your wells.

- Grace builds a wall of protection.

"My grace is sufficient for you, for My strength is made perfect in weakness." 2 Corinthians 12:9

Paul sought the Lord for deliverance from a difficult problem in his life. God answered with this word. The word "sufficient" suggests the idea of "raising a barrier" or "warding off". What a thought! When circumstances around you seem overwhelming--impossible to bear, God's grace is there to protect you, raising a powerful wall of protection or driving away the problem entirely.

"Where sin abounded, grace abounded much more". Romans 5:20b

When you feel sin has locked you behind prison walls you can cry out for more grace. We can never define the limitless grace of God. It will always be "much more" than needed or necessary to set you free from the separating walls of sin and into a fortified place of God's protection.

- Sanctification builds a wall of protection.

The word sanctification means set-apart, dedicate, become holy. Sanctification is like a wall or boundary. It is the sphere of God's love, His protection, and His provision that sets you apart to belong to Him and only Him.

Jesus said, *"And for their sakes J sanctify Myself, that they [that's you] also may be sanctified by the truth." John 17:19*

David knew his boundaries were set and established by God's sovereign plan.

"O Lord, You have searched me and known me. You know my sitting down and my rising up. You have hedged me behind and before and laid Your hand upon me. Such knowledge is too wonderful for me; Jt is high, J cannot attain it." Psalm 139:5,6

The word "hedged" suggests a protective boundary guarding you. You and I can identify with this scripture. I remember feeling a similar emotion the night the Holy Spirit woke me with these words: "Gloria, draw a circle and a dot." Without knowing anything more when I drew the circle and placed a dot in the center I thought, This is so cool. I'm surrounded. Any direction I turn, God has me covered.

Later I learned that Titus 2:14 declares protection for every believer. The word "peculiar" (or special) is pictured as a circle and a dot. The circle is God the Father; God the Son; and God the Holy Spirit providing love, protection, and provision for His own. The dot is you. You are surrounded by His protection.

> *"(Jesus Christ) who gave Himself for us, that He might redeem us from every lawless deed and purify for Himself His own special people (or purify unto Himself a peculiar people)..." Titus 2:14*

- Truth builds a wall of protection.

Truth is something you can stake your life upon- the absolute standard found in God.

> *"Stand therefore, having your loins girt about with truth..." Ephesians 6:14a*

Truth sets you free from the enemy's deception, as well as sin. You must know truth by personal relationship with Jesus Himself who is "the way, the truth, and the life", then you will know the Spirit of Truth, the Holy Spirit who lives in every true believer. His job is to guide you into all truth. (John 16:13)

The devil is a liar and the father of lies. To defeat him you must stand strong for truth--cherish truth--speak truth--guard truth--believe truth.

We are hearing a lot of talk about building a wall to protect our borders. It is such a delicate subject. One thing is for sure and certain, God, Himself protects His own.

Chapter Sixteen

Put On The Lord Jesus Christ

What is the armor of God we are instructed to put on? How do I put on this protective uniform of the army of God?

First of all, the armor of God are invisible, supernatural garments of protection and power given to believers in Jesus Christ. This also includes the robe of righteousness, the garment of praise as well as the full armor of Ephesians 6, designed to protect against every attack of the invisible enemy. (Isaiah 61:3)

In the fortified place of God's love, His powerful protection and abundant provision, there is total and complete victory for those who follow hard after Jesus Christ. Each piece of the "whole armor", is an attribute of Jesus. With His supernatural enablement you will lead a life of victory, being fruitful in the works of God and bringing glory to His holy Name. Isn't that exactly what you want?

How can this become a reality in your life today? It's time to get dressed for war! You will want to be found standing after the battle is over, so let's look at the spiritual weapons in the armor of God at your disposal, as listed in Ephesians 6.

> *"Finally, my brethren, be strong in the Lord and in the power of His might. Put on the whole armor of God, that you may be able to stand against the wiles of the devil. For we do not wrestle against flesh and blood, but against principalities, against powers, against the rulers of the darkness of this age, against spiritual hosts of wickedness in the heavenly places. Therefore take up the whole armor of God that you may be able to withstand in the evil day, and having done all, to stand. Stand therefore, having girded your waist with truth, having put on the breastplate of righteousness, and having shod your feet with the preparation of the gospel of peace; above all, taking the shield of faith with which you will be able to quench all the fiery darts of the wicked one. And take the helmet of salvation, and the sword of the Spirit, which is the word of God, praying always with all prayer and supplication in the Spirit, being watchful to this end with all perseverance and supplication for all the saints." Ephesians 6: 10-18*

We've heard many teachers say when a verse begins with the word, "therefore", you need to ask yourself, what is it there for? In Ephesians 6:13, it is there to remind us there is cause for attention. We are fighting against some really bad guys--actually satan and his hoards of demons (not flesh and blood, but principalities and powers of darkness). We are to war in prayer against these fallen angels and the invisible works of hell and we are called to not only conquer in Jesus' Name, but to be "more than conquerors". Since we are at war it's very important that you have a deeper, clearer knowledge of the armor God has provided.

Picture if you will being in the U.S. Army, standing at attention before your commanding officer. When a command is given with military snap and curtness, you don't have to ask if you should obey or not. A good soldier responds with one quick answer, "Yes sir!" This is the meaning of, "take up the whole armor of God." It is an order to be obeyed at once. As a follower of Jesus Christ you are to take up and put on all the armor of God as a once-for-all act of obedient faith and keep that protective lifestyle active during your entire life here on earth, becoming more and more like Jesus.

I remember when I was first learning about and teaching on the armor of God. I had this image of a Roman soldier in heavy metal armor from head to foot. I couldn't get this out of my mind. I thought I had to put on this heavy armor every morning and take it off when I went to bed. I soon realized I needed more protection during my sleep than I did during the day as I was tormented with burning memories and satan- inspired dreams. That's when I decided I had to keep my armor on all the time. It took a while for me to unlearn some thoughts on what the armor of God is and what it is not. I hope you will find this study helpful so you can be properly equipped with all that God provides for living and for overcoming.

"Stand therefore," reminds us that we are at war. You may have already fought and won many battles, but now you must take your stand for the next attack. You can stand because you are prepared. You aren't naked, but dressed for God's battle, God's way. We do not fight with man's weapons. God has provided powerful, state-of-the-art weaponry for His army. Standing in Christ, with His attributes becoming our way of life brings victory every day.

Truth

"Stand therefore, having girded your waist with truth..." Ephesians 6:14a

The first piece of armor listed is truth, meaning openness, sincerity, truthfulness. This being first should establish the importance of being honest and truthful with God and with yourself.

It is no secret that many times we attempt to disguise our real person as if one can fool God. Being truthful and forthright in relationships and being honest with yourself will protect you and direct you. Isn't that what we learned in kindergarten? Can you remember getting caught telling a lie, or taking something that didn't belong to you? God has been teaching us about this vital piece of protection for life here on earth since childhood. God's truth protects, sustains, directs, and sets us free.

> *"Jesus said...I am the way, the truth, and the life..." John 14:6a*

- Protection -- *"...Let your loving kindness and Your truth continually preserve me." Psalm 40:11b*

- Sustaining -- *"Sanctify them by Your truth. Your word is truth." John 17:17*

- Direction -- *"Oh, send out Your light and Your truth! Let them lead me..." Psalm 43:3a*

- Freedom -- *"And you shall know the truth, and the truth shall make you free." John 8:32*

The enemy is called the father of lies because that's who he has been from the beginning--a liar and a deceiver. Opposing the truth is the strategy of the evil one. He will suppress, corrupt and/or deny God's truth.

> *"For the wrath of God is revealed from heaven against all ungodliness and unrighteousness of men; who suppress the truth in unrighteousness." Romans 1:18*

> *"who exchanged the truth of God for the lie and worshiped and served the creature rather than the Creator..." Romans 1:25*

Righteousness

"...having put on the breastplate of righteousness..." Ephesians 6:14b

"For He (God) made Him (Jesus), Who knew no sin to be sin for us, that we might become the righteousness of God in Him." 2 Corinthians 5:21

The Heavenly Father paid a great price for this transformation to become a reality to all who are born again into the righteousness of His Son.

Being right with God gives you the ability to stand in the Father's presence without fear. You are becoming Christ-like with the nature of God, being conformed to the revealed will of God in all areas. His character is being lived out through you as you think His thoughts, say His words, and do what He would do.

Reminder: All spiritual warfare is victorious only on the basis of appropriating the provision of the cross and Christ's blood given for you.

It is important that you know and embrace who you are in Christ--the righteousness of God. Reject every accusing, guilt producing, shaming thought in your mind. Choose to walk in (put on) the breastplate of righteousness.

"Jesus said, Blessed are those who hunger and thirst for righteousness for they shall be filled." Matthew 5:6

<u>The key to receiving from God is found in your level of hunger or thirst for the presence of the Lord Jesus in your life.</u>

"...put off, concerning your former conduct, the old man which grows corrupt according to the deceitful lusts, and be renewed in the spirit of your mind, and that you put on the new man which was created according to God, in true righteousness and holiness." Ephesians 4: 22-24

Peace

"...and having shod your feet with the preparation of the gospel of peace..." Ephesians 6:15

Having the peace of God gives a believer firm footing. The gospel of peace through the blood of Jesus is the only lasting peace you can experience. Throw off all anxiety or worry. You need the protection of His peace to face the enemy with courage and confidence in the power of God. He is our peace!

"Therefore, having been justified by faith, we have peace with God through our Lord Jesus Christ." Romans 5:1

Faith

"...above all, taking the shield of faith..." Ephesians 6:16a

In addition to all the equipment provided thus far, every believer should add the shield of faith. The word "shield" used here pictures the large, oblong shield of the heavy infantry. Faith in the Lord Jesus is like a protective shield and is needed to assure victory over sin and all demonic attack in a believer's life.

The fiery arrows represent temptations which the enemy continually uses in his attacks. Stand firm in God's goodness and faithfulness.

Reminder: "I trust You, Lord!" should be your favorite four words in the face of disappointment, loss, threats, illness or any attack of the enemy.

Again, remember personal faith that positions itself against evil is victorious because of the blood of Jesus Christ.

"So Jesus answered and said to them, Have faith in God." Mark 11:22

Salvation

"And take the helmet of salvation..." Ephesians 6:17a

The helmet of salvation that a believer is to take is protection from the power of sin and satan in this present life. Salvation is security. You are surrounded by Almighty God and His protection covers you, protecting your mind while you live in this crazy world.

"My sheep hear My voice and I know them and they follow Me. And I give them eternal life, and they shall never perish, neither shall anyone snatch them out of My hand." John 10: 27,28

Christ's salvation is total in scope for the total person: spirit, soul, and body. It is revealed in three tenses: past, present, and future.

1. Past -- When you believe in Christ, you can instantly say you have been saved from the penalty of sin which is death or separation from God. (2 Corinthians 1:19; Acts 16:31)

2. Present -- You are in the process of being saved and delivered from the power of sin as the new nature of Christ grows within us. This is the process of grace in a believer's life. (Romans 8:13; Philippians 2:12; Deuteronomy 7: 22,23)

3. Future -- You will be saved from the very presence of sin at the coming of our Lord or your home-going to Him. (Romans 13:11; Titus 2: 12,13)

The Word of God

"...and the sword of the Spirit, which is the Word of God." Ephesians 6:17b

God's weapon of choice is His Word. No temptation, no accusation, no lie or deception can stand against truth.

> *"For the Word of God is living and powerful, and sharper than any two-edged sword, piercing even to the division of soul and spirit, and of joints and marrow, and is a discerner of the thoughts and intents of the heart." Hebrews 4:12*

As with any weapon you have a choice to pick it up or to leave it. Far too many choose to leave the Word of God on a shelf somewhere collecting dust. Many believers use it as an ornament to dress for church on Sunday morning. This is very dangerous since your sword, God's Word is the most important weapon to use against satan.

Someone has wisely said, "Any response to the Gospel that does not include obedience is self-deception".

Prayer

"Praying always with all prayer and supplication in the Spirit..." Ephesians 6:18

As a believer your great desire is to please the Lord. This means obedient faith is vital. In verse 18, we are given two specific orders.

1.   Pray always.

2.   Be watchful.

"Always", is all the time, at all seasons pray as directed and empowered by the Holy Spirit. It is impossible to be ready for battle, fully dressed in your uniform, God's armor, without constant, sincere prayer. This is the battle!

Praying in the Spirit has these important characteristics:

- It will be according to the will of God. (I John 5: 14,15)

- It comes from a clean heart. (James 5:16)

- It is prayed in full assurance of faith.(James 1:6)

- It is asked in Jesus' name. (John 14:14)

"Watching" is to stay awake, be alert, attentive at all hours. Many believe the body of Christ is waking up. Someone posted that the Lord said, "The alarm has been set but many believers are already awake and preparing." I want this to be said of me, don't you? We can see this happening all around the world. There are more people praying today on Planet Earth than at any time in history. God is waking up His Church. The hour is late. We are at war and the situation is critical. This is no time to be A.W.O.L. (Absent without leave). Stand you watch. The Kingdom of Heaven is at hand.

> *"...It is high time to awake out of sleep for now our salvation is nearer than when we first believed. The night is far spent, the day is at hand. Therefore let us cast off the works of darkness, and let us put on the armor of light...put on the Lord Jesus Christ..." Romans 13:11, 12, 14a.*

Conclusion

So, in conclusion let's ask ourselves, where is my fortified place? The Word of God calls it a mystery, which is a divine secret now being fully revealed to God's people by His Spirit for you to understand and apply to your life.

> *"...the mystery which has been hidden from ages and from generations, but now has been revealed to His saints. To them God willed to make known what are the riches of the glory of this mystery among the Gentiles: which is Christ in you, the hope of glory." Colossians 1: 26,27*

Our goal for the season ahead is to consistently be in the presence of the Lord. In this place of shelter and safety everything you need is found. Stay in your fortified place.

> *"For of Him and through Him and to Him are all things, to whom be glory forever. Amen" Romans 11:36*

More Resources by Gloria Russell

SURROUNDED

BELIEVE BEYOND BASICS

Printed in the United States
By Bookmasters